The Gospel Acco1

You must be born again

Other Titles in the Book by Book Video Bible Study Series:

GENESIS
Video Bible Studies with Richard Bewes, Paul Blackham and special guest Anne Graham-Lotz.
Accompanying Study Guide by Paul Blackham

EXODUS
Video Bible Studies with Richard Bewes, Paul Blackham and special guest Joseph Steinberg.
Accompanying Study Guide by Paul Blackham

PSALMS 20–29
Video Bible Studies with Richard Bewes, Paul Blackham and special guest Stephen Lungu.
Accompanying Study Guide by Paul Blackham

GALATIANS
Video Bible Studies with Richard Bewes, Paul Blackham and special guest Jonathan Edwards.
Accompanying Study Guide by Paul Blackham

JONAH
Video Bible Studies with Richard Bewes, Paul Blackham and special guest George Verwer.
Accompanying Study Guide by Paul Blackham

1 PETER
Video Bible Studies with Richard Bewes, Paul Blackham and special guest Don Carson.
Accompanying Study Guide by Paul Blackham

Coming Soon...

1 & 2 THESSALONIANS
Video Bible Studies with Richard Bewes, Paul Blackham and special guest Rico Tice.
Accompanying Study Guide by Paul Blackham

The Gospel According to John

You must be born again

Authentic

British Library Cataloguing in Publication Data
A catalogue record for this book is available from the British Library

ISBN 1–85078–507–4

Cover Design by Diane Bainbridge
Typeset by WestKey Ltd, Falmouth, Cornwall
Printed in Great Britain by Bell & Bain Ltd., Glasgow

Bethan,
whose diligence, patience and godliness
has carried the work through the hardest
18 months

Contents

Contents

How To Use This Book

BOOK BY BOOK is a video-based Bible Study resource with linked Bible Study questions and a mini-commentary, provided in this Study Guide by the Rev'd Dr Paul Blackham. It has been designed principally for use in small groups, but can also be used for personal study or larger group situations.

Structure of Video and Study Guide:

There is a strong link between the video-based Bible discussions and the written Study Guide to help group discussion and study. Key features provided by the studies are as follows:

- There are 10 x programmes on the video.
- Each programme is 15 minutes long.
- The on-screen host is Richard Bewes, with co-host Paul Blackham. A specially invited guest joins them in the Bible discussions.
- Questions from the video-based discussions are printed at the start of each section of the Study Guides.
- In the Study Guide, there are also Bible Study questions on a selected portion of the text covered in each session. These focus on one short Biblical passage in greater detail.
- There is no 'answer guide' to the questions in the Study Guide – although clearly answers (and applications for daily living as Christians) are provided to questions posed during the on-screen discussions. Answers may also be found in the Further Notes at the back of the Guide.
- The Daily Readings after each Bible Study are intended to give the reader a broader picture of what is going on in each part of the Bible covered in a session.
- There are more detailed notes on each session at the back of the Study Guide. These will be of great help to leaders or anyone wanting to learn more about the particular book of the Bible. (This could also be used in isolation from the on-screen discussions as a mini-commentary.) Further questions are listed at the end of each session.

These are generally more difficult and are possibly of most use to those who would like to study the relevant passages in more detail.

Structure of Group Session:

Please note – the material has been designed in such a way that there is no need for a specially trained leader in order to be able to use the material.

- We would highly recommend that each group member reads the relevant Bible passage prior to your discussion.
- Timing: we estimate that the study session will take about 1 hour. Given the volume of material you may even choose to take two weeks per study – using the questions linked to the video discussions for one week and the Bible Study questions for the next.
- Use of the video programme: for many, simply watching the discussion of the Bible passage may in itself be a wonderful encouragement and learning tool, and your study session may be limited to discussion on this alone. It is entirely up to your group as to whether you watch the on-screen study before or after your own group Bible Study on the passage.
- Prayer: you may want to include personal applications in your group prayer time which arise from the discussions.

Some introductory thoughts from Paul Blackham:

Thousands of small groups are starting up all over the world – but what is it that is going to sustain them? It has to be the Bible. However, so often people don't quite know what to do with these small groups. Meeting together, sharing testimonies and experiences or the odd verse is ultimately too sparse a diet to sustain people's spiritual needs in the long run and really help them to grow.

What is needed is confidence in the Bible, and the ability to be able to go to a book of the Bible rather than just an isolated verse. Each book of the Bible was written with a purpose, and it is only really as we digest it as a book that we understand the real message, purpose, direction, storyline and characters.

It's a lot easier than people often think. You might think, "Oh, I can't manage a whole book of the Bible", but what we're trying to do in BOOK BY BOOK is to break it down and show that actually it's easy.

The Bible was written not for specialists, not for academics – it was written for the regular believers, down the ages.

Introduction

The Gospel of John has so often been the Gospel that is given to non-Christians to introduce them to Jesus. There are good reasons for this.

First, John says that his purpose in writing the Gospel is to help people to trust in Jesus. John 20:30–31 – 'Jesus did many other miraculous signs in the presence of His disciples, which are not recorded in this book. But these are written that you may believe that Jesus is the Christ, the Son of God, and that by believing you may have life in His name.'

Second, John's language and style is very simple and accessible. He uses a simple vocabulary and grammar. Whereas people might struggle with the sophistication of Moses' style or the length of Paul's arguments, John has an apparent simplicity that is encouraging for the newcomer to Bible reading. John chapter 1 is the classic introduction to learning New Testament Greek for this very reason.

So, it might seem that John's Gospel is ideal as a gateway into the Scriptures. However, there is much more to John than is often assumed. Traditionally in the history of the Church he has been called 'the Theologian'. This is not to say that the other Biblical writers are not very theological, but that in John's work there is a direct engagement with the doctrine of God that is equalled only by Moses in the Bible. John seems to approach the question of Jesus of Nazareth through the Biblical doctrine of God, and that can be a much bigger agenda than the casual reader may want to face.

On top of that, the simplicity of John's style conceals a complexity and depth unmatched in the New Testament. Although the words and sentences are simple, the ideas take us into the deepest theological water. The simple concepts of light, life, darkness, bread, water, seeing and hearing are all heavily loaded with the most profound truths the world has ever known.

Finally, John is in many ways a book of Old Testament study. John assumes that his readers are well versed in the Hebrew Scriptures, perhaps to a greater extent than any of the other Gospel writers including Matthew who wrote to convince a Jewish readership. Jesus' actions and words are recorded in such a way that John takes us back to the depths of Hebrew theology. Time after time what might seem puzzling in John becomes clear only when we turn to the Hebrew Scriptures for the full picture.

So as we study John we will find ourselves taken to the basic and central gospel truths of the whole Bible, and yet John will take us deeper into those realities. This Gospel will expand our view of Jesus, showing us again and again that He is the eternal Son of the Father, the divine Mediator over the whole creation, the LORD[1] of the New Creation.

---

[1] We will follow the procedure used in most English translations of the Bible and use the word LORD in capitals where the Hebrew Scriptures have used the name Yahweh.

Video Notes

Session 1

John chapter 1 – Revealing

The following are the questions featured in the video which accompanies this Study Guide. If you wish to, you or your group can use them to recap on what you have been watching. Following this, there is a Bible study on a section of the passage covered by this session which can be used instead or additionally.

1. The Witness of Moses, 1:1–5

Why was John's Gospel written?

What is special about the way in which John begins his Gospel? How is it different from the other Gospels? What is his starting point?

2. The Witness of John the Baptist, 1:6–28

It seems John is very concerned that we should know who Jesus is. How does he present Jesus to us?

We often seem to gloss over the character of John the Baptist, or simply mention him in passing. Are we giving him proper attention?

Verse 18 tells us that no one has ever seen God the Father. It is Jesus who makes God visible. How does He do this?

3. The Witness of God the Holy Spirit, 1:29–36

What is the significance of Jesus being called the Lamb of God?

4. The Witness of the Disciples, 1:37–51

How could Jesus be 'the One Moses wrote about'? John 1:23–34

Bible Study 1

John 1:23-34

1. Who is John and what is his role? See verse 23. Why do you think John is described as the greatest of the Old Testament prophets (Matthew 11:11)?

2. In verse 29 where does the title John gives to Jesus come from (see Genesis 22:7–8)? Why does there have to be bloodshed for sins to be taken away?

3. What reason does John give as proof that Jesus surpasses him (verse 30)? Consider how we can use this proof in our own testimony to Jesus. (Jesus is older than Plato, Buddha, the Egyptian pyramid builders, the druids of Stonehenge, etc.)

4. In verse 31, why did John baptise with water? How did John's baptisms accomplish this?

5. From verses 32–34 what is John's testimony of Jesus, and how does he prove it? How is this eyewitness account helpful to our faith in Jesus?

6. What does the Spirit resting on Jesus in verse 32 show about Him? What implications did this have for His ministry?

7. How would you explain the Trinity from this passage?

Daily Readings:

Session 2

John chapters 2–3 – Teaching

1. Ceremonial Water Jars, 2:1–11

John tells us that the wedding of Cana took place on the 3rd day. The 3rd day after what? Is this just a trivial piece of information?

What is the significance of turning water into wine?

2. Clearing the Temple, 2:12–22

Has Jesus just lost His temper in the incident at the Temple?

3. Born Again, 2:23–3:21

Why do you think Nicodemus came to Jesus? Was he expecting the kind of reply that Jesus gave him?

What does Jesus teach Nicodemus about how he should have understood the Old Testament Law?

4. Ceremonial Washing, 3:22–36

What does John the Baptist teach us at the end of chapter 3 about the identity of Jesus?

Bible Study 2

John 2:1-11

1. What other significant events in the Bible take place on the 3rd day? (Some hints: Matthew 16:21, Matthew 12:40) What has that got to do with this story?

2. Many people think of God as being very far removed from 'real life' on Earth. How does this story of Jesus at a wedding prove otherwise?

3. How do Mary and the servants respond to Jesus? What can we learn from them about our own response to His work and instructions through the Spirit in our lives?

4. This miracle takes place at a wedding. What other wedding is talked about in the Bible? (See Revelation 19:7-9 or Matthew 25:1,6,13). Do you think this helps us to understand Jesus' miracle of transformation?

5. In the Bible, what does wine symbolize? (See Mark 14:24-25)

6. With this in mind, what does John mean when he tells us that this miracle reveals Jesus' glory? (in verse 11) What kind of glory is he talking about?

7. As followers of Jesus, what kind of glory should we be seeking for ourselves? (1 Peter 4:13-14; Jeremiah 9:23-24)

Daily Readings:

Day 1:	John chapter 2
Day 2:	John chapter 3
Day 3:	Matthew 22:1–14; 25:1–13
Day 4:	Malachi chapter 3
Day 5:	Psalm 69
Day 6:	Numbers 21:4–9
Day 7:	Revelation 19:1–10

Session 3

John chapters 4–5 – Working

The following are the questions featured in the video which accompanies this Study Guide. If you wish to, you or your group can use them to recap on what you have been watching. Following this, there is a Bible study on a section of the passage covered by this session which can be used instead or additionally.

1. A New Woman, 4:1–42

How do we see the teaching of Jesus so far in John's Gospel be put into practice in the way He deals with the woman of Samaria?

How does the Living Water change the Samaritan woman?

What does Jesus teach us here about worshipping God?

2. A New Family, 4:43–54

After this encounter with Jesus, we read that the Royal Official and his whole family were changed. Why is this?

3. A New Man, 5:1–15

Why is it important that the healing of the man at the pool of Bethesda happened on the Sabbath day?

4. An Old Work, 5:16–47

How is Jesus the test of all religion or true faith?

Bible Study 3

John 4:7-15

1. Why did Jesus talk to this Samaritan woman? What social and religious barriers did He break through to talk to her?

2. What does this show about the gospel message? What does it tell us about how Jesus looks on every human being?

3. Are there any people rejected by our society or our group of friends who we don't associate with for similar reasons? How can we change this situation in order to bring glory to the Lord?

4. What is the Water of Life that Jesus talks about in verse 14? See John 7:38–39. What does that mean in practical terms for our daily lives? How are we refreshed by this Water of Life day by day?

5. What things in our lives are symbolized by the water of verse 13?

6. How much of our time, money and thoughts are spent on trying to drink the water that will not satisfy us eternally? Compare this to what time and energy we spend drinking the Water of Life. How can we help each other in this area? See Isaiah 55:1–4.

Daily Readings:

Day 1:   John chapter 4

Day 2:   John chapter 5

Day 3:   Hebrews 4:1–13

Day 4:   Luke 9:51–10:24

Day 5:   Luke 10:25–37

Day 6:   Exodus 24:1–11

Day 7:   Isaiah chapter 55

Session 4

John chapters 6-7 – Feeding

The following are the questions featured in the video which accompanies this Study Guide. If you wish to, you or your group can use them to recap on what you have been watching. Following this, there is a Bible study on a section of the passage covered by this session which can be used instead or additionally.

1. The Offer of Resurrection Life, 6:1-15

What is the test that John talks about in verse 6?

2. The Lord of Resurrection Life, 6:16-21

Why is it a very special thing that Jesus can show power over water?

3. The Bread of Resurrection Life, 6:22-71

The crowd seem to misunderstand Jesus again and again. Is this such a difficult teaching about eating the flesh and drinking the blood of Jesus? What does it mean?

4. Killing Resurrection Life, 7:1-31

In chapter 7, the crowd want to kill Jesus. Is it possible that they could have done that right there and then?

5. Spreading Resurrection Life, 7:32-52

How does the last half of chapter 7 show us the worldwide Gospel?

Bible Study 4

John 6:25-40

1. What had the crowd most enjoyed about Jesus' miracle with the loaves and fish? What does Jesus say they should have focussed on?

2. How do the crowd assume they will get this from the Father? Verse 28. In what ways is this response similar to both our own view and the view of our culture for being right with God or 'getting to heaven'?

3. What does Jesus teach us is actually the only way to gain eternal life, verse 29? What action does this require on our part? If we really believe this, how will we live? How will we pray?

4. What **reality** was the manna in the book of Exodus a **shadow** and **sign** of? Why was it not good enough? (Look also at verses 49-51).

5. How do we eat the Bread of Life? How often? How much should this be our focus in life?

6. How are verses 37-40 a great encouragement for us as we try and share the gospel with others?

7. Can you summarize these verses into a simple gospel message? Pray together that you might be able to share this simple message with someone over the coming weeks.

Daily Readings:

Day 1:   John chapter 6

Day 2:   John chapter 7

Day 3:   Exodus chapter 16

Day 4:   Psalm 107

Day 5:   Exodus chapter 3

Day 6:   Joel chapter 2

Day 7:   Acts chapter 2

Session 5

John chapters 8–10:21 – Shining

The following are the questions featured in the video which accompanies this Study Guide. If you wish to, you or your group can use them to recap on what you have been watching. Following this, there is a Bible study on a section of the passage covered by this session which can be used instead or additionally.

1. True Judgement, 8:1–29

How does Jesus deal with the crowd and the woman? What does this show us about the way in which He deals with us?

Why does John organise his material so much around the theme of light and darkness?

You can't have God if you won't have Jesus. Is this message true of John chapter 8? How can we live by this truth in today's society?

2. True Children, 8:30–59

Jesus would have had to be 2000 years old if He had met Abraham. So what does He mean when He says that He has, verse 56?

3. True Sight, 9:1–41

What is the lesson that comes out of the healing of the blind man?

4. True Shepherd, 10:1–21

We move from seeing the truth to hearing the truth in John chapter 10. What is the meaning of these two parables?

Bible Study 5

John 9:1–12

1. It is easy to think that we are being punished when things go wrong in our lives. From verses 1–3, what can we learn from Jesus about how to look on our weaknesses?

2. Can we think of other Bible characters with physical weaknesses? (Look at 2 Corinthians 12:7–10; Exodus 4:10–12) What can we learn from their responses to their situations, and the way the Lord used them?

3. What do light and darkness symbolize? (Remember John 1:1–5, or look at Acts 26:18.) What then is the work of the Father, verses 4–5?

4. It has been suggested that Jesus was using the healing properties of mud to heal the man's eyes! What is the real reason that Jesus uses mud to heal the man? (See Genesis 2:7)

5. Have a quick look at the end of the story in the rest of the chapter. What are we to learn about **true sight** and **true blindness** from the reactions of the man and the Pharisees to Jesus Christ?

6. In what ways does Jesus use the physical situation to point us to the spiritual one? Which is more important?

7. Is this the way we also look on situations surrounding us? Pray that we would keep our focus on Jesus' teachings whilst engaging with the physical world, especially in our understanding of the problems of the world.

Daily Readings:

Day 1:   John chapter 8

Day 2:   John chapter 9

Day 3:   John 10:1–21

Day 4:   Genesis chapter 18

Day 5:   Romans 6:15–23

Day 6:   Romans 2:17–28

Day 7:   Psalm 23

Session 6

John chapters 10:22 – 12
– Dividing

> The following are the questions featured in the video which accom-
> panies this Study Guide. If you wish to, you or your group can use
> them to recap on what you have been watching. Following this,
> there is a Bible study on a section of the passage covered by this
> session which can be used instead or additionally.

1. Seeking His Death, 10:22–42

Why does Jesus quote Psalm 82 to the unbelieving Jews in 10:34?

2. Calling from Death, 11:1–46

How is Martha a good example to us as Christian believers?

How do we see the humanity and the divinity of Jesus in this situation with
Lazarus?

3. Preparing for Death, 11:47–12:11

What do we learn about true motivation from this episode with the
perfume?

4. Going to Death, 12:12–36

What is the significance of the fact that Jesus rode into Jerusalem on a
donkey?

5. Hearts of Death, 12:37–50

In 12:41, John tells us that Isaiah saw Jesus' glory. What does he mean
by that?

Bible Study 6

John 11:20-27

1. In the eyes of the world, who would have more respect, and who would be seen as wise – the Pharisees (Teachers of the Law), or this woman Martha? What about in the eyes of the Lord? What does this teach us about how to treat other people?

2. Why does Martha say verse 22? What does she know about Jesus' relationship to the Father?

3. Look at this same promise **to us** in John 14:13–14. How is it possible that Jesus will do what we ask? What is the purpose of the things we should ask Jesus for, according to these verses? How do we know what these things are?

4. Martha seems to know all about the Resurrection life future and the Final Day. She would only have had the Old Testament to study to find these things out. Where would we look to explain such things from the Old Testament? (example: Job 19:23–27; Psalm 23). It's good to keep a note of such verses as we read through the Scriptures.

5. Verses 25–26 can sound a little confusing. What kind of life, Resurrection, and death is Jesus talking about here? How do we know this?

6. What does the word 'Christ' mean? Why is it so important to the gospel to believe that Jesus is the **Christ**, and the **Son of God** (as in verse 27)? Why isn't it enough to believe He is a good man, or a prophet from God?

Daily Readings:

Day 1:	John 10:22–41
Day 2:	John chapter 11
Day 3:	John chapter 12
Day 4:	Psalm 82
Day 5:	Isaiah chapter 6
Day 6:	Psalm 118
Day 7:	Matthew 5:17–20 & 6:19–24

Session 7

John chapters 13-15:17 - Loving

The following are the questions featured in the video which accompanies this Study Guide. If you wish to, you or your group can use them to recap on what you have been watching. Following this, there is a Bible study on a section of the passage covered by this session which can be used instead or additionally.

1. The only way to receive the New Life, 13:1-20

What is the great lesson to learn from Jesus washing the feet of His disciples?

2. Choose or refuse the New Life, 13:21-38

We often imagine that Judas was a very wicked character. Why didn't the other disciples know that he would betray Jesus?

3. Power for living the New Life 14:1-31

How does Jesus comfort His disciples throughout chapter 14 and prepare them for the time of suffering that is to come? How do these things comfort us now?

14:28-31 have been the cause of some controversy about the identity of Jesus. What is actually being said in these verses?

Some people are concerned that the Apostles weren't able to correctly remember the words of Jesus when they wrote their accounts. How can we be sure that they did?

4. Remaining in the New Life, 15:1-17

What is the fruit that Jesus has in mind for us to bear as branches of the vine?

Bible Study 7

John 14:6–18

1. Many Western Christians struggle with Jesus' teaching in a pluralist society. John 14:6 is a rock against which every human religion is broken, whether it be Islam, Atheism, Buddhism, Judaism, New Age, etc. However, why did Jesus say this to the disciples in their situation?

2. No one has ever seen the Father, but many people have seen Jesus in both the Old and New Testaments. How are we to understand Jesus' words about seeing the Father in verse 7?

3. Why did Philip want to see the Father (verse 8)? What might he have been thinking? Where was he going wrong?

4. In verses 9–11 Jesus explains why He looks like the Father. How would we summarise His teaching here? Why is this unique to Him?

5. Verses 12–15 sound like a blank cheque or an offer of three wishes from a genie! The Father always gives Jesus whatever He asks for because Jesus always perfectly carries out the will of the Father. In the same way, if we are trusting Jesus, helping Him to bring glory to the Father, we will receive all that we ask for. What does this really mean in our day-to-day prayer life? What can we ask for?

6. The disciples knew the Spirit's presence and Jesus promised that the Spirit would remain in them even when He had physically left them (verse 17). How can **Jesus** say "I will come to you" (verse 18) when it is **the Spirit** who is with us?

7. The world will not accept the Spirit because it does not know Him (verse 17). How does this fact affect our evangelism and our prayers for those who don't believe in Jesus?

Daily Readings:

Day 1:	John chapter 13
Day 2:	John chapter 14
Day 3:	John 15:1–17
Day 4:	Psalm 41
Day 5:	1 Peter chapter 1
Day 6:	Romans chapter 6
Day 7:	Acts chapter 2

Session 8

John chapters 15:18–17:26
– Sending

The following are the questions featured in the video which accompanies this Study Guide. If you wish to, you or your group can use them to recap on what you have been watching. Following this, there is a Bible study on a section of the passage covered by this session which can be used instead or additionally.

1. Hatred for the LORD of Life, 15:18–25

How do the words of Jesus in the last half of chapter 15 help us to understand why we face persecution and suffering?

2. Witnessing to the LORD of Life, 15:26–16:15

What is the mission of the Holy Spirit, Whom Jesus promises to us?

3. Joy in the LORD of Life, 16:16–33

What is the joy that Jesus speaks of in chapter 16?

4. Glory in the LORD of Life, 17:1–26

What 'time' or 'hour' is Jesus referring to in His prayer of chapter 17?

What is amazing about Jesus' prayer so soon before His death?

The last part of Jesus' prayer is a prayer for all believers. How does it help us in our evangelism?

Bible Study 8

John 17:20-26

1. In this passage, Jesus is praying for us. Why is it so important that we are to be united as believers? (verses 20–21)

2. Does it surprise us that this is the first thing for which Jesus prays for us? Why? Do we pray this when we pray for other Christians? Do we strive for unity in our church?

3. From verses 21–23, what should non-Christians come to know from the way we love each other as Christians? Do our unbelieving friends know these specific things? How can we make sure that they do?

4. From verse 24, how do we see Jesus acting as the Mediator to bring us to the Father? How close could we come to the Father without Jesus? (See also John 14:6 & 1:18)

5. If the glory of something is its true nature being displayed, what from verse 24 is the glory of Jesus, and from where and how has it come?

6. How does Jesus continue to make the Father known, verse 26? And how is He in us, also verse 26?

Daily Readings:

Day 1:   John 15:18–27

Day 2:   John chapter 16

Day 3:   John chapter 17

Day 4:   1 Peter chapter 2

Day 5:   Galatians 5:16–26

Day 6:   Hebrews 4:14–5:10

Day 7:   Psalm 139

Session 9

John chapters 18-19 - Dying

The following are the questions featured in the video which accompanies this Study Guide. If you wish to, you or your group can use them to recap on what you have been watching. Following this, there is a Bible study on a section of the passage covered by this session which can be used instead or additionally.

1. Binding the I AM, 18:1-14, 19-24

What is surprising about the way in which Jesus is arrested and taken off for questioning?

2. Denying the I AM, 18:15-18, 25-27

How did the event of the denial change Peter's life forever?

3. Judging the I AM, 18:28-19:16

What is ironic about the Jews keeping to the laws of the Passover while they are holding Jesus captive?

In 18:38, Pilate asks "what is truth?" but doesn't stay to hear the answer. How is Pilate an example of living in the darkness rather than in the light?

4. Killing the I AM, 19:17-42

Jesus was thirsty while He was on the Cross. How does this tie in with one of John's major themes?

Bible Study 9

John 19:28-37

1. Jesus has spoken throughout John about the Living Water we can drink (John 4:13–14) to satisfy our thirst eternally. What then does it mean for us that the Fount of Living Water is thirsty? What does this teach us about the Cross?

2. What does Jesus mean when He cries "It is finished"? What things were finished on the Cross?

3. In verse 31 we read of some "Law keeping" Jews. What is ironic about their behaviour? What is the point they are missing?

4. How do you think the Father looked upon their Law-keeping? What similarities can we see between these Jews and people we know who are 'religious' and attend church but do not have a personal faith in Jesus? How can we help people like this?

5. In this passage John is careful to point out the many Old Testament prophecies which are fulfilled in Jesus' death. Why is this important to know?

6. We cannot have Christianity without the Cross. This is the central most vital part of our faith. Can we explain why? Imagine being asked by someone who doesn't understand the death of our God.

Daily Readings:

Day 1:   John chapter 18

Day 2:   John chapter 19

Day 3:   Isaiah chapter 53

Day 4:   Psalm 22

Day 5:   Zechariah 12:10–13:9

Day 6:   Exodus chapter 3

Day 7:   Revelation chapter 5

Session 10

John chapters 20-21 - Living

The following are the questions featured in the video which accompanies this Study Guide. If you wish to, you or your group can use them to recap on what you have been watching. Following this, there is a Bible study on a section of the passage covered by this session which can be used instead or additionally.

1. The Empty Tomb, 20:1-9

We come now to the reality of the power of the Resurrection – what Jesus has been teaching all the way through the Gospel of John. What has the Resurrection of Jesus got to do with the new birth for Nicodemus, the new life for the Samaritan woman, or the new eyes for the blind man?

2. Appearing to His disciples, 20:10-31

What did it mean for the disciples to see Jesus after the Resurrection? What can we learn about the New Creation from these episodes in the room and with the fish in chapters 20–21?

If it is only God Who can forgive sin, what does Jesus mean in 20:23 when He says that the Apostles can forgive sins?

What lesson does Thomas have to teach us?

3. The Miraculous Catch, 21:1-14

What must Peter have thought when he saw Jesus for the first time after his denial?

4. Commissioning Peter, 21:15-25

How does Jesus restore Peter's sense of purpose and affirm him?

What is John's picture of Jesus in his Gospel?

Bible Study 10

John 20:24–31

1. Why didn't Thomas believe the other disciples? Are we to copy him in the way we approach Christianity, or not?

2. Of all the people Jesus could have appeared to, and the things He could have talked about, He chooses here to help Thomas learn a lesson about unbelief. What does this tell us about how the Lord looks on our own doubts and struggles? Are they as unimportant to Him as we might often think?

3. One day we will stand before Jesus and see the scars in His hands and side. How do you think you will feel on that Day? How does it make us want to live our lives differently now?

4. In verse 29, who gets a special blessing and why?

5. Why did John write his Gospel? (verses 30–31) Which part of the book would you use to convince someone of this truth?

6. What is the significance of believing that Jesus is the Christ (anointed one, Hebrew: Messiah), the Son of God? What does that mean for Thomas' statement in verse 28?

7. What has been your favourite part of John's Gospel throughout our studies in this book? What has impacted your life the most? Pray that these things would continue to help you follow Jesus and for an opportunity to share these things with someone else.

Daily Readings:

Day 1:   John chapter 20

Day 2:   John chapter 21

Day 3:   1 Corinthians 15:1–34

Day 4:   1 Corinthians 15:35–58

Day 5:   Psalm 23

Day 6:   1 Thessalonians 4:13–5:11

Day 7:   Revelation 20:11–21:8

Further Notes

John chapter 1 – Revealing

Key Truth: Jesus is revealed to be God the Word, the Son of God, the Lamb of God, the Messiah, the One Moses wrote about, the King of Israel and the LORD God of Israel.

1. The Witness of Moses, 1:1–5

Whereas Luke begins his Gospel by rolling up his sleeves for historical research into the life of Jesus of Nazareth, John begins so very much earlier. We are taken back to a time before anything was created, a time before the history of the universe began. John shows us what existed before there were any humans, angels, animals, or planets. He shows us God and His Word who is also God. These two divine Persons were together[1] before all things.

This chapter of John bombards us with the identity of Jesus. Different witnesses are called who each describe the Person we are about to study. The first witness seems to be none other than the mighty prophet Moses.

It is obvious that John has Genesis chapter 1 open on his desk as he writes his Gospel. He begins with the very same words – 'In the beginning…'. The concepts of the Word, God, the Spirit, creation, light, darkness, life and humanity occupy both chapters. John wants us to see what Philip saw in John 1:45 – 'We have found the One Moses wrote about in the Law.'

As Genesis 1:1 confronts us with the God ('Elohim'[2]) who is a plurality, so John follows Moses' lead in these first verses of John. The Living God

---

[1] With the Holy Spirit of course, as in Genesis 1:2, but in these opening verses John directs our attention simply to Jesus' eternal relationship with His Father.

[2] The Hebrew word *Elohim* is a plural word, though it takes a singular verb. In Hebrew a noun can be singular, dual or plural (for three or more). Naturally the Trinity, *Elohim*, is a plural.

is made up of God, the Word and His Spirit, just as in Genesis 1. Every-thing was created as God the Father spoke through God the Word.[3] In this way, God the Word was established as the centre and source of the whole cosmos (John 1:3–4; Genesis 1:1–4). Everything that exists finds its meaning and purpose in God the Word. Life is **from** Him and **for** Him, and to exist without Him is to miss life itself.

In Genesis 1:3 the darkness is not able to resist the light in any way. As soon as the light shines from the Word of the Father the darkness is dispelled. John picks this up in 1:5. The light still shines but the darkness has still not been able to overpower or resist it. This is not just a statement about the first moments of the universe, but a statement about the on-going relationship between the light of God the Word and the darkness of evil and unbelief in the world. It is a theme that will appear many times in John's Gospel.

2. The Witness of John the Baptist, 1:6–28

John the Baptist was of such historic importance that he was prophesied in the Hebrew Scriptures – Isaiah 40:3; Malachi 3:1; 4:5–6. However, he was sent from God (verse 6), with one task: to witness to the light of God the Word, so that all humanity would trust in Him. John the Baptist was so great, and had so many disciples (see John 1:35; 3:25; Acts 19:1–4) that we have to be warned away from treating him as the Messiah (verse 8). John was simply a **witness** to God the Word, the light and life of the cosmos.

In verses 9–11 we are told the bad news about the relationship between God the Word and the creation. This light has been shining on every member of the human race (verse 9). Even though the whole creation came from Him, nevertheless, the human race has never recognised this light. The world belongs to Him, but humanity has ignored Him.

Nevertheless, verses 12–13, there have been a few people who have trusted in the true light shining in the darkness. They have not been disap-pointed. By trusting in God the Word, they have been given a new birth, a birth into the family of God.

John the Baptist was sent to prepare the way for an amazing event. Verse 14 – God the Word became flesh, one of us, born of the virgin Mary. God the Word made His home among us, within His own creation. The apostle John gives us his own eye-witness account: 'We have seen

---

[3] If a member of a cult tries to suggest that Jesus is a divine **creature** it is good to remind them of this verse. Every single thing that has been created was created through Jesus, God the Word.

His glory, the glory of the Only-Begotten who came from the Father, full of grace and truth.'

The grace, truth and glory of the LORD God of Israel were truly seen in Jesus of Nazareth. There can be no mistake about His identity.

We return to the testimony of John the Baptist – verses 15–18. The key truth that the apostle wants us to grasp is that **Jesus existed as God the Word before He became a fleshly human being**. John the Baptist testified that Jesus is so much greater than John precisely because He existed before John did. It is important to remember that in human terms John was older than Jesus (see Luke 1:1–80). Nevertheless, John wanted people to know that Jesus was far, far older than him.

God the Word is full of grace (verse 14), and it is from His fullness of grace that all gracious blessings have ever been received (verse 16). For example, verse 17, although the Law came through Moses, yet all grace and truth has always been through Jesus Christ. The grace and truth known in Israel was through God the Word.

This is backed up by the proof of verse 18. No-one has ever seen God the Father at any time. This seems to be a reference back to Exodus 33:20 & 23 when Moses asked 'the LORD hidden in thick darkness' if he could see Him – 'you cannot see My face, for no one may see Me and live.' Nevertheless, even in the book of Exodus the LORD is in fact seen – for example in Exodus 24:9–11 – 'Moses and Aaron, Nadab and Abihu, and the seventy elders of Israel went up and saw the God of Israel…' Even earlier, in Genesis 16:13[4], the LORD is seen by Hagar. It was God the Word who revealed the Unseen Father then, anticipating the Word becoming flesh.

'We must carefully remember that none of the appearances of God to man, described in the Old Testament, were the appearance of God the Father. He whom Abraham, and Jacob, and Moses, and Joshua, and Isaiah, and Daniel saw, was not the first person of the Trinity, but the second.'[5]

In verses 19–28 John the Baptist, under investigation by the religious leaders of the day, further reveals the identity of Jesus. John denied that he himself was the Christ or the Prophet[6] or Elijah.[7] Rather John points back to Isaiah 40:3. John is the one who prepares the way for the LORD…

---

[4] See even earlier in Genesis 12:7.

[5] From Expository thoughts on John - Volume 1 by J.C. Ryle. Published by Banner of Truth 1987. Page 42, commenting on John 1:18.

[6] This is a reference to the Messianic prophecy of Deuteronomy 18:18.

[7] Perhaps the religious leaders imagined that Elijah had come back down from heaven in a fiery chariot – see 2 Kings 2. John the Baptist was the fulfilment of the prophesy of Malachi 4:5–6 as Jesus explains in Mark 9:11–13.

therefore Jesus is the LORD God of Isaiah 40. John's work of baptism is nothing more than this preparation for Him (verses 26–27). John had only **water** to pour on people, but Jesus, God the Word, is the One who pours out God the Spirit.

3. The Witness of God the Holy Spirit, 1:29–36

John was able to so accurately and profoundly identify Jesus because of the witness of the Holy Spirit to Him.

John had been sent from God the Father (verse 6), and had been told by Him (verse 33) that he would know for sure about Jesus when he saw God the Spirit descending and remaining on Him. John wants to make it clear that his testimony about Jesus is not just his own personal opinion ('I myself did not know Him'), but that it rests on the authority of God the Holy Spirit.[8] Jesus was anointed with the Holy Spirit, showing Him to be **The Anointed One** (English), The Messiah (Hebrew), The Christ (Greek).

There is a further title authorised by the Spirit that John used of Jesus: 'The Lamb of God, who takes away the sin of the world.' This is one of the very oldest of all the Messianic prophecies in the whole Bible. It takes us right back to Genesis 22. In verse 8, Abraham made an incredible prophecy: 'God will provide Himself the Lamb for a burnt offering.' To fix that prophecy in the history of his people Abraham named the mountain 'Yahweh Yireh' (The LORD will provide), because (Genesis 22:14) 'On the Mount of the LORD it shall be provided'. That Mountain was the very mountain that Jerusalem was built upon, Mount Moriah, the place of Jesus' crucifixion.

4. The Witness of the Disciples, 1:37–51

The chapter concludes with some remarkable testimonies from the disciples of Jesus.[9]

John repeatedly identified Jesus as the Lamb of God of Genesis 22 (verses 35–36), and two of his own disciples decided to follow Jesus because of this clear witness. One of these was Andrew, the brother of Peter. He told Peter, 'we have found the Christ'.

---

[8] John recognised the identity of Jesus before he was even born! See Luke 1:41

[9] In Mark's Gospel, we are shown the lack of understanding and confusion of the disciples. Here in John's Gospel we are allowed to see that however much the disciples misunderstood the mission of Jesus, yet His basic identity was known.

When Jesus told Philip to follow Him (verse 43), Philip told Nathaniel, 'We have found the One Moses wrote about in the Law, and about Whom the prophets also wrote – Jesus of Nazareth, the son of Joseph.' Jesus is **The One** that Moses wrote about in the Law. We are faithful to Moses when we investigate how the ceremonies, laws and arrangements prophesy the Messiah. All the animal sacrifices were enacted prophecies of the prophecy of Genesis 22:14.

This is true of the prophets as well, as Philip tells Nathaniel. They also were writing of **One Person**, the Messiah. The key to the Old Testament is Jesus, God the Word, the Messiah, the Lamb of God.

Nathaniel provides his own testimony alongside Philip's in verse 49. Jesus is the Son of God, the King of Israel. To call Jesus the King of Israel here is much more than a claim that Jesus had royal connections. God the Word is not a king like any of the ordinary kings. In Isaiah 6:1 the great prophet tells us 'In the year that King Uzziah died, I saw the Lord seated on a throne…' The ordinary king of Israel died, but the true King of Israel remained.[10] Jesus is the divine Messiah-King of Israel **before** and **above** and **beyond** all the sinful kings down through history.

The chapter ends with one more testimony, and it is from Jesus Himself – verse 51. He describes Himself as the Son of Man, the link between heaven and earth that even the angels depend upon. The title Son of Man reminds us of Daniel 7:13–14, where the Son of Man holds all authority and power with an everlasting kingdom. However, if we read Genesis 28:10–13 we can see the Scripture that Jesus had in mind. Jacob met with the LORD God of Abraham, Isaac and Jacob, the One who joined heaven and earth together. Jesus indicates to Nathaniel that he will see that reality just as Jacob did.

By the end of the chapter we are gasping. We have received so many testimonies about Jesus' identity we might feel bewildered. He is just too much for us to grasp. He is categorically more than anything we can imagine.

---

[10] Remember that when John quotes from Isaiah 6 he tells us that it was Jesus Whom Isaiah saw in the Temple – John 12:41.

Further Questions:

1. There are so many groups that attack the true divinity of Jesus. Some say that He only began when He was conceived in Mary, whereas others allow Him to be a divine **creature** who existed before the rest of creation. All of these groups seem to agree that 'God' is just one person, usually the Father alone. What is the best way to show the folly of this heresy from the Bible?

2. It is clear already in our studies in John that the Hebrew Scriptures are going to play a very important part in understanding Jesus. The apostles did all their evangelism from the Hebrew Scriptures. Imagine that you were going to explain the gospel of Jesus relying only on the Old Testament. How would you do it?

3. Much of the 'spirituality' that is popular today focuses on the 'natural world'. John wants us to see that all 'creation spirituality' must be about Jesus, God the Word, if it is true to reality. Why is there such a rift in even **Christian** popular thinking between Jesus of Nazareth and the creation? How can we explain to our New Age friends the real nature of 'creation spirituality'?

John chapters 2-3 - Teaching

Key Truth: God the Word, the LORD of Creation, is also the LORD of the New Creation.

1. Ceremonial Water Jars, 2:1-11

Why did the Word become flesh? Why did God the Word, the life and light of the cosmos, make His home among us? What is the business of the visible form of the Invisible God? Not only the wedding feast of Cana, but the cleansing of the Temple and the conversation with Nicodemus in these next two chapters all concern the issue of **Resurrection and New Life**.

The marriage feast at Cana takes place 'on the third day'. This is no simple piece of trivial information. Throughout John's Gospel details about night and day, the time of the year, or the day of the week all are given to tell us how to understand what we are reading. Experiences of new life, new beginnings, 'resurrection' and future hope typically happen on 'the third day' in the Hebrew Scriptures. For example, see Genesis 22:4 with Hebrews 11:17–19. In Exodus 19 it is on the third day that the Unseen LORD in the thick darkness comes to speak to His people from heaven. 1 Corinthians 15:4 reminds us that the resurrection of Jesus from the dead was on the third day according to the Scriptures. This is repeated throughout the New Testament[1].

At the wedding, in response to a request for more wine, **Jesus replies that it is not yet time for Him to die**. It is not yet His 'hour' (NIV 'time'). In John's Gospel this 'hour' refers to His crucifixion, (see John 12:23, 27; 13:1; 17:1). Why does Jesus think about His **death** here? The request for wine causes Jesus to consider the cup of wine He

---

[1] For example, Matthew 16:21; 17:23; 20:19; Mark 9:31; 10:34; Luke 9:22; 18:33; 24:7, 21, 46.

must drink at the Cross, the cup symbolizing the judgement of God.[2] It is not yet time for that, but it **is** a good time to teach what His suffering would achieve.

There were 6 stone jars used for ceremonial washings. Leviticus 11 describes the original ceremonial washings of the Law, showing that every area of life affected by sin was marked out as unclean. Disease, death, mould, decay and the blood-loss of menstruation were all highlighted by the Law. These effects of sin and the curse must not be simply accepted: one day all these problems will be driven out of God's good creation. One day the creation will be reborn and restored.

So, Jesus instructs the men to fill these big ceremonial jars with water. Is Jesus going to perform a major ceremonial wash? He certainly wanted to indicate that He came from heaven to do what all those ceremonial washings were looking forward to. He had come to perform the great washing of rebirth, the New Creation of all things.[3]

Jesus turned all the water into wine, and it was extremely good wine, verses 8–10. **The ceremonial water was turned into the marvellous new wine of the Kingdom.**

By showing the wedding guests that the Resurrection future could happen only through His death and blood, so He showed them His true glory (verse 11) – the 'glory' of His suffering on the Cross, see John 17:1–4.

2. Clearing the Temple, 2:12–22

In Jerusalem Jesus was profoundly angered by the state of His house, the Temple. Through the prophet Malachi, the LORD God had made a specific prediction about the coming of the Messiah to the Temple. The messenger had been sent (Malachi 3:1 – John the Baptist) and now the Messenger of the covenant – the LORD Himself[4] visited His Temple. Just as prophesied, He had come to purge away the corruption and renew all things. Now was the time for renewal and restoration.

It was the Feast of Passover (verse 13). This was the time of recalling the night of the Exodus when Israel was redeemed from slavery in Egypt. Only those who had killed a lamb as a substitute survived the judgement as the Great Angel **passed over** their house. It prophesied

---

[2] In Luke 22:42, as He was about to go to His death, Jesus prayed, 'Father, if You are willing, take this cup from Me; yet not My will, but Yours be done.'

[3] Titus 3:4–5.

[4] The Angel of the covenant is the Great Angel, the Angel of the LORD. See Genesis 16 for more about Him. He is none other than God the Word, the Son, Jesus the Messiah.

that the Lamb of God would cause the ultimate judgement of God to pass over those who trusted in Him. The Passover Feast was one of the key ways that the people of God looked forward to the great renewal and redemption that the Messiah would achieve through His death. Naturally, Jesus died at Passover.

It was supposed to be a time when the **gift** of redemption was freely enjoyed, but instead, the dominant message in the Temple was **buying**. Did they imagine that the Lamb of God **Himself** could be bought and sold! How upset Jesus must have been!

The disciples had probably thought that they were quite devoted to the Temple, but their own apathetic and inactive response to the money-changers showed them how little they really did care. When they saw the Messiah's passion for His Father and the true freedom of the gospel message, they understood what Psalm 69:9 was saying about Him, which they quote in verse 17 of our passage.

When the commotion had settled down, the officials demanded a 'miraculous sign' (verse 18) to prove Jesus had the authority for such action. Needless to say, Jesus would not submit to such parlour tricks. Instead He refers them to the ultimate sign, the thing that would truly mark Him out as the LORD God of Malachi 3:1.

Written into the very structure and layout of the Temple was the message that one day the Lord will live with humanity on a restored Earth. So, when Jesus speaks of destroying the Temple and raising it again in three days, He is telling us that His Death and Resurrection would bring about the very thing that the whole Temple was set up to teach. He would fulfil the prophetic sign of the Temple itself – the renewal of the whole creation.[5]

3. Born Again, 2:23–3:21

Although many people were ready to believe in Jesus (verse 23), nevertheless Jesus knew all too well that the sinful human heart is deceitful and fickle. For example, the man Nicodemus (3:1) came to Jesus with a seemingly flattering speech, but because Jesus knew what was in that man's heart He dealt with the **real** issue straight away.

Nicodemus was a ruler in Israel, and may well have been one of the top theologians of the day (verse 10). He came to Jesus at night, perhaps because he was ashamed of his visit or more likely because his motives

---

[5] If we study the Temple in greater detail, we will understand what Jesus means so much better. For a detailed look at the Tabernacle (the Temple was a permanent version of the Tabernacle) and its message, see the **Book by Book** Study Guide on Exodus.

were perverse. He begins with words of approval, and perhaps he thought that Jesus would be impressed by this. However, Jesus ignores it and focuses on the real issue that 'Israel's teacher' needed to face up to: how can a person, whether they are Jew or Gentile, enter into the kingdom of God?

Unless a person experiences the new birth they have no part in the kingdom of God (verse 3). The human heart is sinful and needs far more than an Abrahamic genealogy or religious affiliations in order to be accepted by the Father, Son and Holy Spirit. There was no way into God's family without entering into the Messiah's Death and Resurrection. As the water changed into wine, as the universe needed to be re-made, so the human heart must also be regenerated – born again.

Nicodemus was taken aback. This was not how he had planned this conversation. What Jesus said didn't seem possible (verse 4). He had never heard of such things.

Jesus did not sympathise. Nicodemus **ought** to know these things. He must have read the Hebrew Scriptures many times, so these things were staring him in the face (verse 7). To be 'born of the water and of the Spirit' is a reference to the new birth or new heart so often offered by the LORD through the prophets.

Ezekiel 36:25–27 – 'I will sprinkle clean water on you, and you will be clean; I will cleanse you from all your impurities and from all your idols. I will give you a new heart and put a new spirit in you; I will remove from you your heart of stone and give you a heart of flesh. And I will put My Spirit in you and move you to follow My decrees and be careful to keep My laws'.[6]

God the Spirit cannot be contained or explained by sinful human flesh (verse 8). He brings the Messiah's new birth without any assistance from the flesh. We see the results of the Spirit's work, but the flesh has no part in it.

Jesus was not giving personal opinions or theories. He was speaking what He knew from first-hand experience (verses 11–13). The testimony of the Father, Son and Holy Spirit is far more weighty than Nicodemus' latest theological fancies.

As if to further test the Scriptural understanding of Nicodemus, Jesus refers him to yet another Messianic prophecy (Numbers 21:5–9). The one place of healing for those bitten by the fiery serpents in Moses' day was the one lifted up on the pole. This was to teach Israel that the Lamb of God had to be lifted up in His death in order to bring healing to the world (verses 14–15).

---

[6] See also Ezekiel 11:19 & 18:30–32; Deuteronomy 10:16; 30:6; Jeremiah 4:4

Nicodemus was the first to hear what has become the most famous verse in the Bible: John 3:16. The whole world stands condemned already because the world has not believed in God the Son (verses 18–19). This, of course, takes us back to 1:9–10 – the light and life of the universe is ignored and the world plunges into darkness. This love of darkness rather than God the Son happens because the world's deeds are evil. We are not innocent victims of an unfortunate situation.

However, if we turn **from** the darkness and our evil deeds **to** God the Word, the light, then we begin to see clearly. Our deeds are now done in and through the Living God, rather than acts of rebellion against Him (verse 21).

We can well imagine that Nicodemus spent the rest of the night in some hard Bible study checking up on the wealth of Bible knowledge in Jesus' teaching.

4. Ceremonial Washing, 3:22–36

Jesus, His family and disciples spend some time in the country, where His disciples baptised some people (see 4:1–2). John and his disciples were also baptising in the region (verse 23). A certain Jew, presumably someone of note, provoked a discussion with John's disciples over this ceremonial washing. All the washings and ceremonies of the Law were given to prophesy and floodlight the Messiah. To spend time on the mere **sign** of regeneration when the Giver of New Life was standing among them was ridiculous.

John reminded his disciples that his mission had always been simply to testify to the Christ. He never claimed to be the Christ himself. He had the great honour of being 'the best man' for the Bridegroom (verse 29), but the bride is for the Bridegroom not for the best man. If Israel went to Jesus in true faith, then his purpose was fulfilled.

The theological profundity of verses 31–36 show the greatness of John the Baptist. John has to diminish next to Jesus because Jesus is God the Son who has come down from heaven. John's origin was the earth and he can only speak on that level. Jesus has seen and heard the realities of heaven, and His teaching is at that supreme level.[7] He has come from eternity in face-to-face contact with the Father in heaven and He speaks what the Father knows. Yet, and this takes us back to the deep darkness

---

[7] Notice John thinks that Jesus not only came from heaven but remembered what He had seen and heard in heaven before He was conceived in Mary's womb. Rather than try to imagine a psychological model to contain such wonders, let's just worship the utter glory of God the Word who became flesh.

of the human heart, 'no one accepts His testimony' (verse 32). John is one of those who accepted Jesus' testimony and thereby affirmed the truthfulness of God the Father. The teaching of Jesus is from the Father and to deny it is to call the Father a liar. The reason that Jesus always knows the words of His Father is that He is the Messiah, **the Anointed One**, Who is given the Spirit without limit. He is not simply a person whom the Spirit **visits**: He is the true **home** of God the Spirit. The Father and Son are united in the fellowship of the Holy Spirit.

God the Word is not at all like John the Baptist or Moses or Isaiah, all of whom were simply servants of God. God the Son is the One through Whom the Father acts, and the Father does not do anything except in and through Jesus, (verse 35). All the Father's business and teaching is in the hands of the Son. The Father refers all His affairs to His eternal Word. **Therefore**, it is scandalous that no-one accepts His testimony and it is no surprise that the Father is so deeply angered by the way we treat His wonderful Son.

Further Questions:

1. We have seen that the ceremonial washings of the Law were an enacted prophecy of the new creation work of the Messiah. What other examples of this kind of 'prophetic washing' can you find in the Scriptures? For example, think about the Flood from Genesis 6–9.

2. So much of the Bible is concerned with the Tabernacle/Temple. It has been suggested that this 'model of reality' should be a standard evangelistic tool in our day-to-day witnessing – that is, we should explain the gospel through the Tabernacle. What do you make of this idea? Can any difficulties in our understanding and presentation be overcome?

3. If new birth is a radical change in us, a brand new beginning in 'what we are', where exactly does this change take place? Is it a change in our minds (our thinking), or is it a change in our bodies or in our spirits? Some might say it is a holistic change in everything that we are, but how does it affect our bodies right now? What part of a person has moved over from death to life? Is it just that we have a radically different **destination** but that we are personally unchanged? Some have said the new birth is the beginning of a process of change in us, but does the language of Jesus fit this kind of view?

Session 3

John chapters 4–5 – Working

> **Key Truth:** God the Word, Jesus Christ, is the only One Who can transform broken and sinful lives through new birth.

1. A New Woman, 4:1–42

Jesus **had** to go to Samaria (verse 4), not because it was on His journey, but because He **had** to bring new birth to a woman there. The woman had come to get water, so Jesus asked for a drink. The woman was surprised- not only was it odd for a man and woman to talk like this (see verse 27), but because Jews did not associate with Samaritans. Nevertheless, Jesus gets to the real issue beyond all social and religious debates: would she receive God the Word? (Remember John 1:10–13). Would this woman become born again as she trusted in the Lord of new creation?

The 'gift of God' of verse 10 is the Holy Spirit, as Peter explains in Acts 8:18–20. The 'Living Water' is another way of referring to the Spirit (we can see this from John 7:39). However, the woman heard Jesus on a trivial level: 'can you dig a well better than Jacob?'

Jesus again offers her the new creation life of the Spirit (verses 13–14). Physical water has to be continually consumed and sustains us only until we die. The Water of Life brings new birth into eternal life, life that can never die because it is destined for the New Creation.

> We must constantly remind ourselves that when we read about 'eternal life' in John's Gospel we should be thinking of **Resurrection life**, **new birth** and the **New Creation**. When we read John 5:24–29, 6:40 and 6:54 we can see what John means by 'eternal life'. We should **not** be thinking about a merely 'spiritual' dimension to life. Eternal life overflows from now to our Resurrection future.

Jesus knew that this woman did not yet fully understand her need of the Water of Life, so He exposes her life. She had been in many relationships. Undoubtedly she was a victim of philandering males, but Jesus exposes her own guilt, her own worship of sexuality (verses 16–18). Her evil deeds had blinded her to God the Word who had given her life and light, and who now stood in front of her.

Did she turn back to the darkness as she tried to side-track Jesus with ancient theological debates (verses 19–20)? Jesus knocks aside such questions with a further presentation of eternal life. The issue of geographical locations for worship are not (and never have been) fundamental. The Father is not looking for people who can get to the right geographical location. He is looking for those who have received what Jesus described in the previous chapter – 3:5–6. The Father seeks worshippers who are born of the Spirit.[1]

With wonderful kindness and grace, Jesus simply tells her that He was the Messiah, and all her doubts and darkness are gone. She just races off to the town to share her new-born life with everyone else. Her witness was tentative (verse 29) perhaps because she wasn't used to this kind of conversation with her neighbours. Nevertheless, the reality of her new birth so impressed them that they all came out to see and trust in Jesus the Messiah.

The disciples were more concerned about their own food than this woman's new birth, but Jesus is sustained by more than the next meal. All His tiredness and hunger disappeared as He revelled in the joy of the New Creation. If Moses could go for 40 days and nights without food or water when he talked with the LORD on Sinai[2] then it is no surprise that the food of Jesus is to do His Father's will, to perform the work of redemption, to grant Resurrection life to the world (verse 34).

2. A New Family, 4:43–54

When someone **hears** or **sees** Jesus, we have to investigate whether they **truly see** or **hear**. For example, in verse 44 John tells us that Jesus knew that a prophet has no honour in his own country, then in verse 45

---

[1] NOTE: sometimes people treat the word 'spirit' as being the opposite of bodily or physical. Thus they read verse 24 as saying that God is the opposite of bodily or physical life, as if our problem is being physical or having bodies. John 3 has defined 'spirit' for us as 'being born again'. We must not forget that it is the bodily, physical God who says God is spirit!

[2] Exodus 34:28.

the Galileans give Jesus a warm home-coming welcome. They saw what He had been doing, but had they really **seen** what He was doing?

A royal official's son was ill (verse 46). Coming from the spiritual darkness of king Herod's social and political world, we might imagine this man to have no chance of being born of the Spirit. However, this man knows that Jesus has the power to grant new life to his dying son (verse 47).

Jesus fears the worst (verse 48). Wasn't this man simply thinking and acting by the flesh? Did he understand that life was **not** about postponing the death of the body, but about being joined to God the Word? The royal official was not deterred by Jesus' challenge. Some English translations have the man say 'sir', but the Greek word is 'Kurie'- Lord. It seems better to translate his plea as '**Lord** come down[3] before my child dies.'

> Christ gave an answer of peace. Christ's saying that the soul lives, makes it alive. The father went his way, which showed the sincerity of his faith. Being satisfied, he did not hurry home that night, but returned as one easy in his own mind. (Matthew Henry).

When he discovered that the new life had come to his boy exactly when Jesus spoke, the official's whole family believed in Jesus.

3. A New Man, 5:1–15

When Jesus engaged with one particular man at the pool of Bethesda (house of mercy), Jesus' overwhelming desire to bring new life is evident from His words to the man: (literally) 'Be raised! Raise up your bed and walk!' From the emptiness and death of a life cut off from the Lord, the man is commanded to **be raised**, almost 'come to life!' Immediately the man was restored. His outward physical restoration was a sign of his new birth. Again, John gives us the clue to what has really happened to this man when he tells us it happened on the Sabbath day (verse 9).

Because the Sabbath is all about entering into God's rest it is always the sign of New Creation hope – see Psalm 95:11 and Hebrews 4:1–11.[4] The fact that Jesus healed the man on the Sabbath shows us that He was focussed on His work of redemption. To bring new creation to this man, through both new birth and bodily healing, was true Sabbath celebration.

---

[3] Literally, 'descend'.
[4] When we compare Exodus 20:8–11 and Deuteronomy 5:12–15 we can see the two themes of creation and redemption in the Sabbath. We look **back** to the original Sabbath rest of creation, but now because of sin we must look **forward** to the Sabbath rest of redemption. Whenever we read of the Sabbath in Scripture we need to think about it from this perspective.

However, those in darkness did not see it that way (verses 10–15). They were so unable to distinguish between sign and reality that they were more interested in the form of the shadow – the Sabbath laws – than the concrete reality of the New Creation standing among them. Instead of being amazed and joyful that a man had walked for the first time in 38 years, they were angry that he was carrying his bed-roll! The man thought that the Lord who healed him surely had authority to tell him to pick up his bed-roll. How could Jesus be doing the works of His Father if He was teaching heresy?

Jesus met the man later and told him that he was **whole** (verse 14). The man had spent his life trusting in mere physical healing at the pool, a life of unbelief and darkness. It was time to stop this sinning[5]. Now that the man had received new life from Jesus, he had to turn away from fleshly confidence and live in the Spirit. The man obeyed Jesus and immediately went back to the spiritually blind Law-worshippers and testified to the power and goodness of Jesus Who had made him whole.

4. Old Work, 5:16–47

The man's faithful testimony did not lead to new birth among the enemies. Rather, they came to find Jesus to sort Him out on the matter of the Sabbath (verse 16). They were about to hear exactly what the Sabbath was really all about.

They seemed to reject Jesus' miracle of new creation because they thought that perhaps even God the Father does not work on the Sabbath. Jesus confronted that foolishness straightaway (verse 17) by confirming that the Father is always at His work, **the work of redemption**, including on that Sabbath day. But, further (and this is what really offends them) Jesus is doing the same work. They grasped Jesus' words (verse 18). If the work of the Father is the work of Jesus, then He is equal to the Father and must be God the Son.

Rather than back down, Jesus explained the relationship between the Father and the Son in great detail. The Son has no agenda of His own, no private work to do. He only does what the Father is doing, and the Father so loves the Son that He includes the Son in everything that He does (verses 19–20). Just as the Father has always been at work, so has the Son. The Father has the power of Resurrection, yet it is the Son who exercises this power for the Father (verses 21–22).[6] It is Jesus who determines who will be resurrected to life in the New Creation and who will be

---

[5] Remember that in John's Gospel, sin is fundamentally a matter of failing to believe in Jesus – 16:9; 3:36.

raised to eternal punishment in Hell. Nobody can have any relationship with the Father unless they love, trust and honour the Son (verse 23).

There are two 'times' in verses 25–29, one that is now and one that is still to come. The **time that is now** is the time when the dead hear the voice of the Son and come to life. Here Jesus speaks of the new birth that happens when people trust Him. The Father has given the administration of life to the Son. There is a **time still to come** when the dead will hear the voice of the Son (verse 28). According to the testimony of the Father, verse 32, Jesus will call all who have physically died back to physical life, and judge between them. Such truths place Jesus the Son at the very centre of reality.

The Father's testimony about the Son is utterly reliable and sparklingly clear, but they have never heard His voice or seen His form and they do not know His words, verses 37–38.[7] If they would trust in Jesus **then** they would come to know the Father, understand His testimony about the Son and look forward to seeing Him in the New Creation (see Matthew 5:8).

They seemed to trust in the **Scriptures themselves** for eternal life rather than the One the Scriptures spoke about. They were more worried about offending **the Law** than the One that Moses was writing about in the Law (1:45). They refused to come to God the Son to receive eternal life. Jesus knew the state of the human heart (verse 42). Its darkness is exposed by its preference for anyone other than the true Sent One, the Angel of God.[8]

---

[6] The work of the Father and the Son is the work of redemption. This is so very important in our own understanding of work. The activities we will be able to enjoy and pursue when we enter into the Sabbath rest of the New Creation will be wonderful as we explore and enjoy the creation as it was always intended. However, the number one item on our agenda right now, as we await the return of Jesus, is the work of redemption. We can never find our purpose in life in our careers. If we attempt to do so we will find redundancy and retirement very traumatic. Our purpose in life is to share the truth about Jesus. That is why the Father has given us places to work and live, sending us to people who may never hear about Jesus other than through our witness. Gospel witness is what we must all 'do with our lives'.

[7] This takes us back to chapter 1:18. When we read the Hebrew Scriptures it is clear that many people not only hear the LORD speaking but also see Him. He **appeared** to a variety of people. Nevertheless, the Father has always accomplished all His work through the Son. That is why the Old Testament appearances of God are often referred to as 'Christophanies' – appearances of Christ before He became flesh.

[8] Angel simply means 'messenger' or 'sent one'. Notice how Jesus loves to define Himself as 'the One sent from the Father'. This is not a New Testament title, but an Old Testament one. The Angel of the LORD or the Angel of God is a

Even though all judgement is in the hands of the Son, yet He makes one concession to the unbelieving Jew who has put their trust in the Law of Moses (verses 45–47). On Judgement Day when every human being is raised from the dead by the voice of Jesus, He will allow Moses to point the finger at those who have trusted in him rather than the One he wrote about. If they were not prepared to believe Moses who spoke so simply and clearly in earthly terms, how would they understand Jesus Himself Who speaks of heavenly mysteries? (verse 47). Moses is the key to understanding Jesus.

The mission of God the Word as the Lord of the New Creation was shown in the lives of a Samaritan woman, a royal official and a crippled man. Nevertheless, instead of the darkness of unbelief dissipating, the darkness deepened and the persecution of the Messiah had begun in earnest.

---

[8] (continued) a title for God the Son used especially (though not exclusively) in Genesis, Exodus and Judges. See for example Genesis 16, Genesis 48:15–16, Exodus 3 and Judges 2:1–4.

Further Questions:

1. The true Son is received with joy and love by every sincere heart. The world is full of people who claim to love God, who claim to be sincerely seeking for the truth about God, yet it is so often shown up as a lie when they encounter Jesus. They reject Him. How do we confront this rejection of Jesus? What is the best way to take such 'searching for truth' seriously whilst holding up Jesus?

2. Imagine that you are talking to someone who follows Moses but not Jesus. Put together your case to show that the teachings and practices written by Moses were all about Jesus the Messiah. How were the ceremonies prophesying the Messiah?

3. Many lives have been ruined by Christians promising miracles that only the Holy Spirit can deliver. He is sovereign in these matters and we need more humility in depending on Him. As we consider the man at the pool of Bethesda what is the place of physical healing in Christian mission? Is our emphasis on 'natural' medicine or 'supernatural' miracles, or neither?

John chapters 6–7 – Feeding

Key Truth: God the Son is the food of Resurrection life. When we believe in Him we eat the Bread of Life and receive new birth.

1. The Offer of Resurrection Life, 6:1–15

In Exodus 16:4, the LORD provided manna to sustain the Israelites in the wilderness. It was a kind of miraculous bread, which was rained down from heaven. In this, the LORD tested the people to see what they really wanted, whether they understood what their **true food** was. In John 6:6 we see the same LORD applying the same test: where can we get food for so many people? **What food do these people really need**?

It is important that we understand Jesus' test. **Jesus did not want the disciples and the crowd to trust that He could miraculously provide lots of physical food for them**. That is exactly what the crowd will believe about Him in this chapter (verse 26) and it is definitely not what Jesus wanted. He wanted them to see the feeding as a sign of His ability to give them new birth, eternal life, a Resurrection future.

In John 6, the same truths are taught as were taught through the manna in the wilderness. In giving the manna, the LORD was asking His people to be satisfied with **Him** as the One who would take them to the New Creation on Resurrection Morning[1]. He was the true Bread from heaven, the food that gave them eternal life. If they would find their satisfaction in Him then the hunger, thirst, persecution or weariness of the wilderness were of no ultimate concern.

---

[1] We can see this from a closer study of manna and how it was to be collected, in Exodus chapter 16. There was to be no collecting on the Sabbath day. Instead, the people were to enjoy the Sabbath rest – a prophecy of the eternal rest of the New Creation.

2. The Lord of Resurrection Life, 6:16–21

While Jesus was on the mountain the disciples go out onto the water in the evening. The waters grew stormy, it was dark and they did not have Jesus with them. Water has great significance in the Bible. There are two aspects to it: **creation** and **judgement**. We are reminded of both aspects in 2 Peter 3:5–6 – "…long ago by God's word the heavens existed and the earth was **formed** out of water and by water. By these waters also the world of that time was deluged and **destroyed**."

The power over water is the power of creation and judgement, and the whole Bible has enormous respect and awe for the LORD God's ability to master the waters. In the oldest book of the Bible, Job acknowledges the unique ability of the Living God to walk upon the water (Job 9:8) – "He alone stretches out the heavens and treads on the waves of the sea." Perhaps especially relevant here is the crossing of the Red Sea in Exodus 14. Between the Passover and the question of bread from heaven, the Angel of God causes the waters of the Red Sea to divide allowing His people to cross over on dry land. Those waters both judged the Egyptians (Exodus 14:23–28) and gave a new beginning to the people of God (Exodus 14:29–31).

When Jesus walked to His disciples on the water, He showed Himself to be the LORD of creation and judgement. **He is the LORD God who can judge the old world and bring in the New Creation**. They were, rightly, terrified by Him (verse 19). It is only when He spoke their fear away (verse 20) that they wanted Him to join them in the boat. As soon as He is with them, the journey over water is accomplished.

Jesus showed His identity when He said: "I AM[2] – do not be afraid." 'I AM' (Hebrew: YHWH – Yahweh) is the name of the Angel of God who met Moses at the burning bush in Exodus 3. When Moses asked for the name of the LORD Who had appeared to him, he was told (Exodus 3:14) **"I AM WHO I AM**. This is what you are to say to the Israelites: '**I AM** has sent me to you.'" We will see that Jesus calls Himself by this name throughout the book of John. He constantly shows us that He is the very same Person Who was at work in the book of Exodus.

3. The Bread of Resurrection Life, 6:22–71

Although the crowd had seen Jesus miraculously feed them, they had not (truly) **seen** the miraculous sign (verse 26). Far more important than merely temporary food is the food that will give us eternal life (verse 27) – a life that will ultimately give us immortal bodies. Jesus will give the food

---

[2] The NIV translates this Old Testament name of the LORD as the simple 'it is I'.

of Resurrection life to us, and God the Father Himself directs everybody to obtain life from Jesus. See how the crowd focussed on how to **work** to get this food from the Father in some other way than Jesus, verse 28. Jesus again replied with the simplest and clearest answer. The only thing that God the Father wants from anybody is that they trust in Jesus.

In verse 35, Jesus says "I AM the Bread of Life." By deploying His divine name from the book of Exodus, Jesus wants them to see that He is and always has been the One beyond and beneath the manna. **He is the reality and everything else is the shadow. Everything else leaves us hungry and thirsty because it is just a shadow**. When we eat this Bread (i.e. trust in Jesus Himself) then we pass from the old creation death into the new creation life.

In verses 52–58, Jesus made it impossible for them to hide from Him behind the Law or shadows. Jesus' words force a choice between a trust in the Law itself or a trust in the One prophesied by the Law. Since Noah in Genesis 9:4 and then Moses in Leviticus 17, the eating of blood was expressly forbidden. Look at Leviticus 17:10–12: "Any Israelite or any alien living among them who eats any blood – I will set My face against that person who eats blood and will cut him off from his people. For the life of a creature is in the blood, and I have given it to you to make atonement for yourselves on the altar; **it is <u>the</u> blood that makes atonement for one's life.** Therefore I say to the Israelites, 'None of you may eat blood, nor may an alien living among you eat blood.'"

With such Scriptures in mind, the words of Jesus in John 6 are wonderful and challenging. **All the laws forbidding the consumption of animal blood were testifying to the blood of the Messiah, the Lamb of God**. His blood must stand alone. The blood of mere animals could never give new birth into the New Creation. The blood of animals could only ever testify to the true blood. All other food and drink is a mere sign and shadow of this true food and true drink (verse 55). **If "the life of a creature is in the blood", then we must drink the blood of God the Word if we are to have His life in us (verse 57)**. The life of the Father is in the Son and will be in us if we feed on Him.

Let's catch our breath. So far in John, to receive eternal Resurrection life we must eat **bread**, drink **blood**, consume human **flesh** and take in living **water**. What does it all mean? What exactly must we do? This is exactly what the disciples were thinking (verse 60). How do we eat the flesh and drink the blood of Jesus? It is as we trust Jesus, listening to and obeying His words, that we receive life. Unlike Judas, Peter acknowledges this truth (verse 68).

4. Killing Resurrection Life, 7:1–31

God the Word had been **offering** His life to the world, but chapter 7 begins with those who wanted to **take** His life. What tragic irony! It wasn't yet time for Jesus' glory[3] (verses 6,8), so He waited in Galilee to avoid the murderous plans. However, when the time for celebrating the Feast of Tents arrived, Jesus went up to Jerusalem.[4]

The atmosphere of debate and hostility towards Jesus pervaded Jerusalem (verses 10–13). This is where He had cured the lame man on the Sabbath in chapter 5, and the issue was still buzzing around (see 7:21–24). Finally, halfway through the Feast, Jesus went to the Temple and began to publicly teach. When His opponents questioned the source of His teaching, Jesus repeated His basic mission statement: He was simply repeating what God the Father had told Him, doing only what the Father willed (verses 16–18). Anyone can discover the truth of Jesus' words if they also obey the will of the Father. Jesus receives honour from the Father, because He always does what the Father sends Him to do.

In verse 19 we return to the testimony of Moses. It is clear that they did not listen to Moses because they were trying to kill the very Person that Moses wrote about (1:45). They might have thought that their passion for Law-keeping was their way of keeping the Law, but their hatred of the Holy One of Israel shows that they were fighting against its true purpose. The purpose of the Law was to bring people to trust in Jesus the Messiah.

When Jesus exposed the intentions of their hearts, shining His light into the darkness, they reacted with hostility. They accused the Messiah, the One filled with the Spirit without limit, of being **demon**-possessed! (verse 20) The crowd was still worried about His miracle at the pool of Bethesda, because it had been done on the Sabbath. How can Jesus be the Messiah if He goes against their (mis)understanding of the Law?

They were happy to re-interpret and adjust their view of the Sabbath for the sake of circumcision, verse 22. Circumcision was seen as **so** important that it could over-rule Sabbath Law. However in their view, the LORD of the New Creation, prophesied by the Law, was not allowed to bring new creation on the Sabbath! They trusted in circumcision more than the Lord who gave circumcision to Abraham. Circumcision was a sign of the new birth (Deuteronomy 10:16; 30:6). The **sign** of the new birth was given preference over the **reality** of new birth.

---

[3] Remember that throughout the Gospel the glory of Jesus is specifically His death on the Cross. See John 17:1–4.

[4] We read about the Feast of Tents (or the Feast of Tabernacles) in Leviticus 23:33–44, and Numbers 29:12–40.

5. Spreading Resurrection Life, 7:32–52

In verses 35–36 the crowd continue to deny Him. Where could He go that **they** could not go? Was He going to run away to the Jews living among the Gentiles? Or, did He want to teach the Gentiles?

Their suggestion is too exciting for Jesus to be silent about. As the **Cosmic** Word, the One who had appeared to Abraham when he was still an uncircumcised Gentile, it had always been His purpose to bring all the nations into Israel, into the Church. The purpose of Israel had always been to bless all the nations (see Genesis 12:1–3).

What a wonderful cry in verses 37–38 as the Fount of Living Water offers Himself to the whole world! John tells us that He cried out on **the last day** of this important Feast.

The Feast of Tabernacles was the feast when Israel understood itself as a nation. Throughout it, 70 offerings were made, symbolically, for all the people of the world. On the final day of the feast just one bull was offered, to show that all the nations find their unity in the one people Israel, the Church of the Living God.

So, when Jesus shouted for the whole world, both Jews and Gentiles, to come to Him for the Holy Spirit, the fact that He did so on the last and greatest day of the Feast of Tabernacles is of profound significance. The crowd was critical of the idea that Jesus might be interested in teaching the Gentiles, and Jesus proclaims that the whole purpose of Israel and its Messiah, God the Word, is to be the international, multinational people of the New Creation.

When John says in verse 39 that "the Spirit had not yet been given" we mustn't misunderstand him. The Spirit had always been present and at work **in Israel**. Throughout the Hebrew Scriptures we see the Spirit at work in His people (see for example Genesis 41:38; Exodus 31:3; 35:31; Deuteronomy 34:9; Judges 3:10; 6:34; 11:29; 2 Chronicles 15:1; Nehemiah 9:20, 30; Psalm 139 etc.) In John 3 Jesus urged Nicodemus to be born of the Spirit and was surprised that Nicodemus did not know all about this. In John 14:17 Jesus says that although the world does not know the Spirit, the disciples **did** know Him. In Luke 2 Simeon was full of the Spirit as he waited for the Messiah (Luke 2:25–26).

Nevertheless, the universal outpouring of the Spirit on **all flesh** could not happen until the Word-made-flesh had been crucified, destroying not only the power of sin, but also breaking down every barrier between Jew and Gentile (see Ephesians 2:14–18). The Cross has made it possible for both Jew and Gentile to have access to the Father **by the Spirit** as equals. Gentiles no longer have to be become Jews in order to be saved.

The prophesy of Joel 2:28–32 explains that very event: the pouring out of the Spirit upon **all flesh**, even on the nations outside of Israel.[5] On that day "**everyone** who calls on the name of the LORD will be saved."

If we look at Young's Literal Translation of verse 39, we get a better understanding of the Greek here: "…and this He said of the Spirit, which those believing in Him were about to receive; for not yet was the Holy Spirit, because Jesus was not yet glorified." The context of the whole passage is the inclusion of the nations within Israel, so perhaps we should understand Jesus' words about the Spirit in the same way. **The Holy Spirit had not yet come to the Gentiles, because Jesus had not yet been crucified**.

The crowd once again reacted wrongly to Jesus. With a loud voice He had offered Himself to the world as the Fount of Living Water, the LORD God of Israel who calls in the nations. The crowd, in the darkness, decide to have another discussion about who He might be.

---

[5] See Acts 2 for the fulfilment of that prophecy.

Further Questions:

1. There are 7 'I AM' sayings in the book of John. Can you identify these? What is the significance of Jesus using the Name 'YHWH' (Yahweh) at these times?

2. Look at the responses Jesus has from various people throughout chapter 6 to His teaching on the Bread of Life. (Verses 41–42; 52; 60; 66; 67–69) As followers of Jesus, we too will experience similar reactions from others. What is our godly response and how do we persevere without giving up? How can we learn from Jesus?

3. Jesus' loud cry of 7:37–38 took place on the last day of the Feast of Tabernacles. Throughout the feast the 70 bull offerings were made, symbolically, for all the people of the world. Look at the total number of animals offered until the last day (see table below). In Genesis 10 we see the whole world divided up into 70 nations. What significance could the number 70 have in the Bible? Where else does it appear and why?

	Bulls	Rams	Lambs
Day 1	13	2	14
Day 2	12	2	14
Day 3	11	2	14
Day 4	10	2	14
Day 5	9	2	14
Day 6	8	2	14
Day 7	7	2	14
Total:	70		
Day 8	1	1	7

Session 5

John chapters 8–10:21 – Shining

> **Key Truth:** Jesus is the light of the world, but humanity is blind in the darkness of unbelief.

1. True Judgement, 8:1-29

When the Pharisees bring a woman they had caught in adultery in front of the crowd, straightaway we are concerned. According to Leviticus 20:10, "If a man commits adultery with another man's wife – with the wife of his neighbour – **both** the adulterer and the adulteress must be put to death." It is true that sin is worthy of death and the Law imposed the penalty of physical death upon a whole variety of sins in order to show the fatal seriousness of all sin. However, if these Law teachers really cared so much about the Law, where is the man? If she was caught in the very act of adultery, he must have been known to them. There is no concern whatsoever for the Law here, and still less for the Messiah referred to in the Law. Their question was simply a trap for the One Moses wrote about (verse 6).

Jesus responded by writing on the ground with His finger. Much ink has been spent on trying to determine exactly what He was writing. The key thing here is that if John wanted us to know what it was he would have simply told us. Was He giving them a chance to think about what they were doing? Perhaps He was writing a relevant Scripture.

After they continued to question Him, Jesus straightened up and got to the central issue. They had dragged the woman in front of the crowd as if sin was her problem alone, something that **she** had fallen into. The fundamental truth that we have learned throughout John is that **every** human heart loves the darkness and hates the light. It makes no difference whether people are 'respectable' about their sin, dealing in arrogance, hypocrisy, self-righteousness and greed, or if people are 'crass' about their sin, dealing in promiscuity, drug abuse, lying or violence.

Judging **ourselves** according to the criteria of social acceptability is one of the deepest and most dangerous traps of all.

The Pharisees had come to trap Jesus, but showed themselves to be trapped in the deceitfulness of the darkness. Their own sin was hidden from them as they abused the Law to condemn others. The Law, above all else, urged them to trust in the Promised Messiah – but they had turned it into a way of justifying themselves and condemning others.

Jesus could have thrown a stone at the woman. He was without sin (2 Corinthians 5:21). Would He condemn her and make her sinfulness an example to others? Of course not. As Jesus taught in John 3:17, He had not been sent into the world to condemn it, but to save it. So, as with the healed man in 5:14, Jesus told the woman to stop sinning. When He said this He was not thinking specifically of her adultery, because even if she became a celibate single for the rest of her life, her life would still have been a life of foul and evil sin if she did not trust and love God the Word. **Sin, according to John 16:9, is ultimately just one thing: refusing to trust Jesus**.

Now the offer of salvation that He had made to the woman He made to the whole crowd. Here we encounter another of the great 'I AM' statements of John's Gospel, verse 12. This language takes us right back to chapter 1:1–5. God the Word who has always been the light and life of the world made a promise to the human race in its treasured darkness. If we will follow the light of the world, He will take us out of the darkness and give us the light of life, the life of the Father which flows through the Son to the world. If we listen to the teaching of the Father and go to the Son, He will save us from the darkness and remove our condemnation. He will bring us into His life, through the new birth.

But, the leaders of the darkness were not about to give up their precious darkness so easily. They again (ironically) try to use the Law against Jesus, verse 13.[1]

Jesus would not discuss His Father with the darkness (verse 19). Nobody knows the Father until they know the Son. All talk about the Father is mere hear-say, opinion, speculation and idolatry until a person has trusted in the Son and received new birth from the Spirit. The rest of John 8 will continue this theme in detail.

The crowd refused to believe Jesus when He made His identity clear to them, verse 25, so He looks forward to the Cross as the moment when the full, undiluted glory of the Living God would stream out to the whole creation. In the darkness of the Cross the light of the world shone most brightly of all.

---

[1] Interestingly, because they have misused the Law in this way Jesus calls it '**your** Law'.

The death of God the Word is the final judgement upon humanity. When we tell others about this sacred mystery we must never become complicit in the unbelief of the darkness, by trying to 'make it reasonable' or 'acceptable'. This event can never be either reasonable or acceptable to us as long as we remain in the darkness hating the light. Only when a person seeks to do the will of the Father can they acknowledge the truth about Jesus (John 7:17). The Cross is the acid test. When we consider the death of the Lamb of God, our true nature as children of light or children of darkness is exposed. As far as Jesus was concerned it was His being lifted up on the Cross that demonstrated to the world His true relationship to the Father. Is the Cross the heartbeat of our life, the ever-exciting centre of our worship?

2. True Children, 8:30–59

In verse 34, Jesus explains about the power of sin. It corrupts and controls. Because we are slaves we have no place in the family of God. The Son, however, has the full freedom of the family. So, the Son has authority to grant freedom to the slaves. As Abraham's descendants the crowds ought to have been the very first to love and trust God the Son, but when Jesus spoke the truth He was not believed. Lies are preferred to truth, just as the devil desires.

Notice that Jesus says they **claim** the Father as their God, but (verse 55) they do not know Him at all. These were devout Jewish people with ancient religious traditions and complex daily rituals. They had a passion for the Law and firmly resisted the pagan religions of the heathen. Surely, if there was any religious group who knew the Father it must be this one? Nevertheless, Jesus' words to the group were very clear and unambiguous. They did not know the Father and their claim on Him was empty. They trusted in their genetic connection to Abraham and not in the Promised Seed that Abraham trusted in.

On the other hand Jesus does know the Father and is **the** keeper of His words. Abraham understood this and behaved accordingly. Abraham rejoiced at the thought of meeting God the Word. He looked forward to it, and when it happened he was glad (verse 56).

There were several occasions in the life of Abraham when he saw God (which according to John 1:18 must have been God the Word and could not have been God the Father). In Genesis 12:7 the Lord **appeared** to him. In Genesis 15:1–5 Abram seemed to meet with a person called the Word of the Lord. In Genesis 17:1 the Lord **appeared** to Abram again, but if we are looking for an occasion when Abraham was filled with joy and excitement, Genesis 18 seems the most likely candidate. There we see the LORD plus two angels visit Abraham and Sarah to eat a meal with them. When we read that story it is clear that Abraham was very glad about the visit.[2]

The crowd hear Jesus and cannot contain their indignation, but instead of backing down or down-playing His words, Jesus takes the conversation up to an even higher level. When He said "before Abraham was born I AM", Jesus was showing that He was also the Angel of the LORD who spoke to Moses at the burning bush in Exodus 3:1–6! Here in John 8:58 Jesus told them the truth: that was **His** name. He was far greater than both Abraham and Moses, because He was the LORD God who spoke to those two great figures of the Hebrew Scriptures.

3. True Sight, 9:1–41

Chapter 8 centred on Jesus as the light of the world who shines with the pure clear light of the Father's words, works and will. In chapter 9, John's camera turns to look more closely at the spiritual blindness of the human race. Every person in the world is illumined by the light of the world (1:9), yet the world wilfully gropes around with eyes tightly closed.

Jesus came across a man blind from birth, verse 1. There must have been something strikingly disturbing about the man's condition because the disciples cannot deal with it (verse 2). They are even driven to the ludicrous position of imagining that either his parents had sinned so perversely that their **child** (not **them**) was punished with the loss of his eyes or the man sinned so badly that he was retro-actively punished with the removal of his sight in the womb! It is difficult to decide which of these is the most heretical.

Nevertheless, this foolishness lurks in us all. That spiritual blindness makes many of us feel that when we are in good health it's because we deserve to be, and that when we suffer we have either been treated unfairly or have **earned** our suffering because of the lack of our works of righteousness. The devil always wants us to imagine that life and eternity is in our own power if we do the 'right things'. Here, once again we are amazed at the tender patience of Jesus. Instead of laughing derisively or exploding with anger at their blasphemous suggestions, He calmly rejected their proposals and told them the truth, verse 3.

For the disciples, like us all, the outward physical condition of the man seems so terrible. With such a problem, surely he was in an unbearable condition. Jesus rejected this analysis. The eyes that the crowds have

---

[2] There is a more in-depth analysis of the encounter of Genesis 18 in the Book by Book Study Guide on Genesis.

used to look at Jesus have been of no value to them at all, because they simply ran deeper and deeper into darkness. If the disciples recoiled from the man born blind, how must Jesus have felt when He could see the horror of our much more terrible spiritual blindness. To have no physical eyes is a burden, but to have no spiritual sight, no true sight of reality... that is so very, very much more horrific because it will take us into the endless darkness of Hell.

Having given this bigger perspective on the man's blindness, Jesus went on to give a sign of His ability to cure the much more serious blindness that we all need to be cured of. His method of healing involved spitting on the ground in order to make some mud for the man's eye sockets. Commentators have drawn attention to the other time that God the Word bent down to form human flesh from the mud or clay, in Genesis 2:7. Just as we were originally created by God the Word (John 1:3), so we can all be re-created by Him through new birth.

What must it have been like for a man who had never known what physical light was to suddenly receive perfect physical sight? It is no wonder that there is such a major public enquiry in the rest of the chapter.

This blind man obviously had not seen any of Jesus' miraculous signs, but he immediately trusted and obeyed Jesus without question or hesitation. The Pharisees who dominate the rest of the chapter had seen what Jesus could do and yet refused to believe in Him or trust Him. The lesson about true sight and real blindness couldn't be clearer.

There is a wonderful, straightforward simplicity and honesty about this ex-blind man throughout the chapter. Around him everybody finds Jesus very complicated, difficult and controversial. The man **sees** with perfect clarity the truth about Jesus: He can deliver the healing that He said He could. Jesus is a man who can be completely trusted.

When thrown out by the Pharisees, verse 34, Jesus found the man. Although he trusted in Jesus, yet he needed more focus. When Jesus explained that He was the glorious Son of Man from Daniel chapter 7, the man is eager to believe it. He calls Jesus "Lord" and worships Him (verse 38).

4. True Shepherd, 10:1-21

Taking up the idea of perceiving the truth, Jesus moved to the model of **hearing**.

The language of the shepherd and his sheep is locked deep into the Biblical story. The LORD God is the Shepherd of Israel (e.g. Psalm 23:1, 80:1). Many of the key Biblical characters were shepherds (e.g. Abel, Jacob, Moses and David). The sheep would have been understood immediately as the members of the nation of Israel (e.g. Psalm 100:3). The Shepherd of Israel is the Messiah, according to Zechariah 13:7.

Jesus described Himself with two 'parables'. He is the gate into the sheepfold (verse 7) and He is the Good Shepherd (verse 11).

In the first, the Pharisees, together with the other leaders of Israel, intend only evil for the sheep. They claim to be shepherds, but they are nothing but thieves and robbers. **Far from wanting to greet the true Shepherd, they wish to keep Him away from the flock**.

In verses 7–10, we have a new and more direct parable of the sheepfold. In this one Jesus is the **Gate** into the sheep pen for the sheep to come in. The sheep that come into the fold through Him are safe and will be properly cared for. The others, the thieves and robbers, do not offer safety at all. They bring only death and destruction. They might **claim** that they know the way to safety and life, but actually they simply want to lead the sheep to the nearest abattoir. Jesus is the good Shepherd as opposed to all the bad so-called shepherds. The hired hand stands for those who are supposed to be watching over the sheep but in the end value themselves more than the sheep. This role is amply filled by the Pharisees.

The **genuine** sheep of Israel recognise the Shepherd. This recognition is not a trivial kind of knowing - verse 15. **The sheep know the Shepherd in the way that the Father and the Son know one another**. There is an experiential and intimate quality to this relationship. The sheep are bound to the Shepherd and He to His sheep, so much so that He will die for them. The Shepherd does not have a variety of different sheep pens for all the nations of the world - there is just One Shepherd for all and one sheep pen for all. Israel, in its true and original sense, is the sheep pen for the whole world and the Shepherd of Israel is the Shepherd of all those in the world who enter through Him.

Further Questions:

1. Jesus dealt with sexual immorality in a way that seems so different to the Church down through history. There is a perfect combination of personal compassion together with holy purity in Jesus. Jesus tackled the social problem of prostitution by both befriending the prostitutes and turning their lives around as they trusted in Him. Though He is the Righteous One, He did not present Himself as self-righteous. Discuss different ways we can put this example into practice.

2. "Jews for Jesus" is a worldwide evangelistic organisation dedicated to showing Jewish people that Jesus is the Jewish Messiah. How do the arguments of John chapter 8 relate to that mission?

3. Jesus said that He wanted to bring sheep from all over the world into His one flock, Israel (John 10:16). Today there are hundreds of millions of Gentile followers of the Jewish Messiah, Gentile members of God's Israel. What should we think about the suggestion that God has two different flocks/peoples, Israel (for the Jews) and the Church (for Gentiles)?

John chapters 10:22–12 – Dividing

Key Truth: Jesus is the Resurrection and the Life. He is the dividing point between light and darkness, life and death.

Throughout the previous chapters we have seen the increasing divide between those who learn from the Father and those who love the darkness. In the next chapters this theme comes to the front. The division between light and darkness reaches a fever pitch when Jesus most graphically demonstrated His ability to grant Resurrection life.

1. Seeking His Death, 10:22–42

In verse 33, the Pharisees were pretending to be deeply upset at the very idea of 'a mere man' having any kind of divine title. They were acting as if God and humanity could never be joined together. Because their trust was in the Law they were very far from the Living God, so far away that even when He was standing right in front of them they refused to acknowledge Him. The god of their hearts and minds was a god who stayed at a distance and gave them instructions to carry out, but **that** god had nothing to do with the real God of the Bible. So, Jesus takes them back to the Scriptures to show them that the relationship between the LORD God and humanity is not what they thought.

Psalm 82 challenges all formal and distanced views of the Living God. The LORD God stands in the middle of the assembled people of God, calling them to share in His life.[1] From this Psalm He shows them that

---

[1] The first verse has been translated in many ways, but the literal meaning of the Hebrew would be: "God stands in the congregation of God ; in the centre God gives judgement." The 'congregation' is the word used many times to refer to

sharing the life of God is the whole point of the life of Israel. Not only is Jesus truly God, but He is also able to bring the rest of humanity into the life of God. If Israel can share in the divine life, then of course the Son does!

In verses 40–41, Jesus finds many people who trusted in Him, because of John's faithful witness. John was the greatest of all the prophets, not because of miraculous wonders – because he didn't do any – but because he so faithfully prepared the way for Jesus the LORD.

2. Calling from Death, 11:1–46

Jesus announced that the illness from which Lazarus was suffering would not end in death and stayed where He was for two more days (verse 6). He knew that Lazarus would die, but only set off on the **third day**. (Remember, the **third** day often signifies a Resurrection experience.) The glory of God in the Son would be revealed through Lazarus' death.

Jesus must have been so refreshed by the depth of Martha's genuine faith shown through her amazing trust in Him, verses 21–27. So, He uttered another of His great 'I AM' sayings. Jesus is the Lord of Resurrection and life. Whoever trusts in Jesus will be raised to life in the New Creation at the end, and will never face the shadow of death ever again (verses 25–26).

Mary's grief, however, deeply moved Jesus (verse 33). Here we see His true divinity. Humanity is so hard-hearted, so indifferent to the last enemy – death. **We** compromise so easily with the fallen state of the world, accepting death and pain and evil and injustice as simply natural aspects of creation. God the Word is always so much more disturbed by the power and destruction of sin. He cannot simply stare dispassionately at the ruin that we have brought on ourselves and His creation. When He saw that His friends had been so traumatised by death, He was 'deeply moved'.

Then, overcome with the grief of His friends and the tragic mess of human sin and death, the mighty eternal Son **wept,** verse 35. Sometimes people have imagined that God is beyond all emotion, above the kind of feelings that humanity experiences. There is perhaps a noble intention in such imagination, hoping to keep 'God' clear from the sins and corruptions of fallen human emotions. However, Jesus shows us what the **real** affections and emotions of God are like. Too often our feelings are small and unreliable, easily moved and changed by small matters. But in Jesus we see true grief and compassion, love and anger and joy.

---

[1] (continued) the family or assembly of Israel, particularly in the writings of Moses.

Death and decay had always had their way with humanity. Now one Man was about to begin the death of death. He commanded the tomb to be unsealed (verse 39) even though Lazarus' decomposition was well under way. To resuscitate a person who has been dead for a few minutes or an hour is one thing; to confront death and decay in a man that had been decomposing for four days in a Mediterranean climate belongs only to the Lord of Resurrection and Life.

When the stone was removed Jesus made a public prayer to His Father (verses 41–42), to show the whole crowd that what He was about to do was done **only because Jesus was sent by the Father and did exactly what the Father told Him to do**.

3. Preparing for Death, 11:47–12:11

In chapter 12, Jesus returns to Bethany, the place where He had called the decomposing Lazarus out of the tomb. He seemed to be loved and trusted here, because a dinner was held in His honour.

Judas Iscariot cared nothing for the love, worship and honour that Mary showed for Jesus when she anointed His feet with her expensive perfume. Judas remained in the darkness and all he could see from the situation was a disgraceful waste of money. If it was worth a year's wages it was a seriously expensive item and Judas was bitter that he did not get a chance to embezzle that money. The fundamental idol of Judas was **money**. When he agreed to betray Jesus, he did it for the money (see Matthew 26:14–16). At the end of the day money was worth more to him than the Living God who could give Him everlasting life in the New Creation.

Jesus would not tolerate Judas' filthy and evil comments defiling Martha's beautiful act of worship. He explained that Mary's actions were absolutely right. She had been saving that precious ointment for the time of His burial (verse 7 and see also Matthew 26:12). We have seen the godliness and understanding of these two sisters, so we should not be too surprised to see that Mary actually knew that Jesus' hour, His time of glory, was very close at hand. **If** Judas was really concerned for the poor he could care for them at any time, but this time of preparing Jesus for death was unique to the whole of eternity.

While this was happening a large crowd had gathered, not only to see Jesus but also to inspect Lazarus. Lazarus was living and breathing proof that Jesus was the Lord of the New Creation, the Resurrection and the Life. These were people who wanted to see the signs and believe in Jesus to receive eternal life.

There is something so chillingly cynical and twisted about the chief priests in verse 10. Lazarus had been brought out of death, but they only wanted to send him back because so many people understood the meaning of the sign and trusted Jesus. These mafia thugs, to protect their own thing, put out a contract on Lazarus.

4. Going to Death, 12:12–36

With so many children of the Light gathered at Bethany, Jesus set out for the short journey (11:18) to Jerusalem. The great crowd began to gather around Him and seemed to be welcoming Him as the LORD God on His way to the Temple. The crowd had turned to Psalm 118 in their celebrations. This was no accident. That Psalm had originally been written as a prophecy of this very day, the day when the LORD Messiah would go up to the altar in the Temple.[2] The Psalm describes to us what these crowds in Jerusalem were doing with their palm branches: "with boughs in hand, join in the festal procession up to the horns of the altar." The crowd also identified Jesus as the King of Israel. Perhaps they did this partly because Jesus rode into Jerusalem on a donkey, just as the prophet Zechariah had predicted in Zechariah 9:9. However, it was only when Jesus was actually crucified on the Friday that they fully grasped the significance of all that they had been quoting from Psalm 118. The Psalm told them that they were escorting the Lamb of God to His sacrificial death, but it seems they didn't fully see it until it actually happened.

Jesus' heart was agitated or frightened as He faced this most terrible death, verse 27. His death was the death of infinite God-forsakenness, the death of Hell and wrath. For everlasting ages, infinite time, the Son had always unquestioningly carried out the Father's will instantly, and yet, here, we are faced with the abyss which is the death of the Son. Throughout John He had constantly defined Himself as the One who simply carries out the Father's works and words. Now, for a moment He contemplates asking the Father for a different will! Can we read these words without trembling? We feel stunned by the Son's divine transparency. And yet, in His great wisdom, honesty and love, God the Word was ready to share even this possibility with us, so that when we fear the future, when we flinch at what the Father asks of us, we find the Lamb of God right there next to us in full and deep sympathy. When we tell Him of how shaken we are about following Him in the way of the Cross, we will not meet an unmoved Mover, but a crucified God who will stay with us and

---

[2] Jesus tells us that Psalm 118 speaks directly of Him in Mark 12:7–12; Luke 20:13–19 and Matthew 21:37–42.

carry us through the very worst if we will be as honest with Him as He has been with us.

Such was the momentous nature of this struggle and victory that for only the third time in the history of the universe, the Father's own voice is heard from heaven.[3] The Father is so thrilled with His Son, so utterly overjoyed at the faithfulness and obedience and love of His only-begotten Son that He has to respond to His request, verse 28.

The Cross is the 'judgement on this world' (verse 31) because it is God's verdict upon this world in its darkness and death. The devil's power lies in the darkness and the Cross is the final and infinite 'NO!' to the darkness.

5. Hearts of Death, 12:37–50

Surely the way to demonstrate the reality and truth of Jesus to the world is through mighty and miraculous signs? If only people could see the unmistakable power of the Messiah, then wouldn't they all believe? How could these crowds have seen Lazarus walk out of the tomb and still think about murdering Jesus? John seems to address these concerns in the rest of chapter 12 as he explains to us the dark and terrible truths of the human heart.

Isaiah the prophet knew all about the hardness and darkness of human-ity. He had spent a lifetime uttering the most wonderful prophecies about the Messiah who would come to die for the sins of His people. From the virgin birth of Jesus (Isaiah 7:14), through His Spirit-filled ministry (Isaiah 11:1–4; 42:1–4) to His death as the Suffering Servant (Isaiah 52:13–53:12), the prophet Isaiah had faithfully pointed the nation of Israel to their Promised Messiah. However, Isaiah marvelled that so few believed what the LORD had told him to say, verse 38. We might feel the same way about friends or family who have heard the gospel message yet do not receive it. Here we are told why.

Notice from verses 39–40 that the choice for darkness has conse-quences. Those who had witnessed the miracles of Jesus could not stay as they were. The Living God gave them over to darkness every time they made that choice. He abandoned them to their love every time they turned from the light. He hardened their hearts and blinded their eyes even further as they refused to see the light who stood in front of them.[4]

---

[3] The other two occasions were on Mount Sinai at the giving of the 10 com-mandments (see Deuteronomy 4:12–15; 32–36) and the baptism of Jesus (see Luke 3:21–22).

[4] Romans 1:21–24 expresses this very same point speaking of the whole human race: "For although they knew God, they neither glorified Him as God nor gave

Their thinking was constantly judged by the Father and as they continued to refuse His Son, so He continued to hand them over to the darkness.[5] We cannot reject the message, the light, with impunity. We cannot walk away from Jesus without being corrupted and deadened by our actions. The Living God watches and judges. **If He does not open blind eyes, then our blind eyes never open**.

Chapter 12 ends with Jesus' final evangelistic appeal to the nation (verses 44–50). There is such simplicity and clarity here. No-one in the world could miss the point of these words. Nobody in the world could be confused as to what they needed to do to receive eternal life. We only need to trust in Jesus, His words and actions, in order to receive this eternal life from the Father.

---

[4] (continued) thanks to Him, but their thinking became futile and their foolish hearts were darkened. Although they claimed to be wise, they became fools and exchanged the glory of the immortal God for images made to look like mortal man and birds and animals and reptiles. Therefore God gave them over in the sinful desires of their hearts…"

[5] We could again compare Romans 1:28 – "…since they did not think it worthwhile to retain the knowledge of God, He gave them over to a depraved mind…"

Further Questions:

1. John 12:23–26 shows us a deep gospel truth hidden in the life-cycle of a seed. Every time we see a seed planted, germinate, grow and produce more seeds, we are witnessing a 'creation sermon' about the death and Resurrection of Jesus. How should we use such 'creation sermons' in our own witnessing? Can we think of other examples of the creation bearing witness to the cosmic Christ? (father-son relationships; sunrise; marriage; the healing properties of plants, etc.)

2. 'Being like God' was the offer of the serpent in the Garden of Eden, and it remains at the heart of human sin; our evil desire to take the place of the Father, Son and Holy Spirit. Many New Age cults and pagan religions talk about humans becoming divine. However, Psalm 82 challenges this with another vision of 'being like God', a vision of being part of the divine life through the divine Mediator. How can we share the divine life so completely? How does Jesus bring us into the life of God?

3. How should we express this awesome Biblical truth, first to a New Age pagan who believes that they are **already** divine and then to a 'believer in god' who doesn't think that their god can have anything to do with humanity?

John chapters 13–15:17 – Loving

Key Truth: Love is at the very centre of Eternal Life: the love of the Father and Son for each other and us; **our** love for each other and them.

As John focuses our attention on the last few hours before Jesus is crucified, we enter into one of the most moving parts of the whole Bible. Here we find Jesus behind closed doors with His closest friends, teaching them about His forthcoming death, demonstrating what that death means, promising them the gift of the Holy Spirit and encouraging them to remain true to Him. The promised new **life** available by believing in His name will mean **death** for the eternal Son. Once again we marvel at the life and work of our Saviour. Like the disciples, we have no part to play. We can only sit back and watch the drama unfold as the very life of the eternal Trinity is shaken by the Cross.

1. The Only Way to Receive the New Life, 13:1–20

The Passover Feast was imminent. The time of His death was at the very door. What would Jesus do to give His disciples understanding of what was about to happen? Jesus shows the character and extent of His love for the disciples by **washing their feet**. We know that the greatest display of His love for us is in the Cross (1 John 3:16) – but this foot washing shows us the **personal** character of His love so clearly. It is possible to see the Cross simply as a legal transaction that is done on our behalf, as if it were almost a dispassionate, impersonal deal. But, before Jesus goes to the Cross, He carefully washes the feet of each of the disciples.

Jesus was well aware that Judas had never received re-birth from the Lamb of God. But, in spite of knowing this tragic and bitter truth **Jesus washed the feet of the man who was about to betray Him to torture and death**.

This incident was yet another mighty sign revealing Jesus' identity and mission. He was the One sent from the Father to **serve**. He was the Suffering Servant. He is the One whose great authority comes from the fact that He served the most. When He washed their feet, they were being asked to acknowledge that they must be washed by Him, that He must serve them. Peter, in verse 8, however, reacts like all the people living in darkness have acted. They will not allow the Holy One of Israel to perform His great work for them.

Peter was clean because he had been born again (verse 10). He needed to keep close to Jesus for the daily cleansing of forgiveness, but the fundamental issue was resolved. He had passed over from death to life, from darkness to the light.

But isn't it interesting that **Judas** does not object to the foot washing? Peter objected but Judas did not. Judas received that awesome sign of new birth, yet in his heart he utterly rejected all that the sign told him. This must remind us that we can receive the most wonderful tokens of gospel reality, whether they be the Lord's Supper, baptism or Church life, **yet** we may still fundamentally reject all that the Light of the world offers to us.

From verse 13 Jesus unravels the full implications of what He had just done. In the kingdom, amongst Christians, **authority flows from service**. The one who is the greatest is the one who serves the most, who does not throw their weight around. We show that we depend on Jesus because we serve one another. When Jesus has set us free from self-service we serve others and know the joy of the kingdom.

2. Choose or Refuse the New Life, 13:21-38

After such an act of service and humility, Judas was trying to figure out how best to kill God. Verse 22 is a solemn verse. None of the other disciples suspected Judas. Sometimes in religious art he is portrayed as a graphically evil man, with his face caught in a greedy sneer. That is to miss the dark mystery of Judas Iscariot and human sin. We always want to portray evil as something that is not like us, something grotesquely different to our 'normal' life. But that is not what real evil is. Real evil is what happens when we do not trust in Jesus the Son of the Most High, and it finds a very welcome home in the most respectable, handsome, polite, gifted and stylish people, just as easily as everybody else. That is why Matthew 26:22 is so striking: "And they were exceeding sorrowful, and began **every one of them** to say unto Him, Lord, is it I?"[1] They

---

[1] I have used the King James Version here, which seems to capture the mood best.

all knew that there was more than enough in each of them to raise the question. We must never think of Judas as insane or from another race of creatures. Judas is one of us, with the same human heart and mind.

Verse 27 is so disturbing. The choice still lay open (in theory) for Judas even when Jesus offered the piece of bread to him. The moment Judas took the bread Satan personally took possession of him. Just as Jesus was one with His Father in fully accomplishing the Father's will, so Judas was one with **his** father fully accomplishing **his** father's will.

The moment of His death marks the time of His departure back to the Father's presence. Although He would see the disciples again after His Resurrection, yet He would not live with them as a regular public citizen of this age again. They would no longer travel around Israel together, or spend time at Bethany or Cana enjoying parties, or confront the opposition of the Pharisees together. That was all coming to its end and within a few weeks He would ascend bodily to His Father for at least 2000 years. So, the teaching of Jesus for the next 3 chapters is all directed to preparing these disciples for His absence, for service in the life of Israel as it goes out around the world.

His first command He describes as a **new** command, verse 34, and yet there is nothing new about what He commands (see Leviticus 19:18). They are to love each other as Jesus had loved them. The mark of the followers of Jesus, even after He had left them, would be their love for each other, their imitation of His great, sacrificial love for them. Peter would later have a great deal to say about this life of love when he wrote his letters (1 & 2 Peter).

Jesus knew that this hour was **so** dark that none of the disciples could stand with Him in that furnace of hostility. He would be utterly alone at the last, abandoned by even these faithful disciples. The hour of His glory would be so dark and terrible that only the eternal Son of Man could endure it. So, Jesus prophesied that Peter would abandon Him and deny Him before morning.

3. Power for Living the New Life (14:1–31)

Nevertheless, Jesus did not want to create alarm and fear in the disciples. Verse 1 is very special. The very word that was used to describe the way in which Jesus' heart was troubled in 13:21 is the word used here when He comforts His disciples telling them not to let their hearts be troubled. Remember how Jesus comforted His troubled heart in 13:31–32? He refreshed and re-iterated His total confidence in His Father to achieve all that He has promised to Him. This is exactly what Jesus recommends to the disciples now. They are to trust in God and their troubled hearts will be calmed.

In seeing Jesus the disciples see the Father. Because Jesus acts and speaks in perfect conformity to the Father's will, so to meet with Jesus is the same as meeting with the Father. Philip seemed to completely miss this and asks for a direct vision of the Father. It is no wonder that Jesus seems hurt by Philip's request. Jesus is the One to Whom the Father has entrusted everything. All authority and judgement belong to the Son and He is one with the Father. Philip sounds almost as if he thought of Jesus as nothing but an introduction to the **real** God, Who is the Father. Jesus takes him back to first principles. To see the Son is to see the Father. There is nothing in the Father that is not in the Son (verse 10). The Father does His work only in and through the Son.

Often people have taken John 14:14 and seen it as a blank cheque for them to claim from Jesus whatever they what, whatever will suit their own agenda, whether it be money, possessions, career, relationships or status. However, that is an abuse of all that Jesus has been teaching. He will grant such total support **NOT** to those who are engaged in **their own work**, but those who do what He is doing – the work of redemption. When we make extravagant prayer requests for ourselves it is always good to return to these verses to ask: how is this the work of Jesus and how is it focussed on bringing glory to the Father? Verse 15 is the wonderful summary statement of all this: if we love Jesus then we do what He commands, we submit ourselves to His will and work. In such circumstances He longs to give us more than we ever dreamed or imagined for the work.

Jesus gives His Church a very specific help in doing His work and bringing glory to the Father: the Holy Spirit (verse 16). If Jesus, the Father's Representative[2], is going away from the disciples, Jesus will make sure that they are fully supported by the other Representative, the Holy Spirit. The disciples know Him already. They have been born of the Spirit and have been caught up in the works of the Spirit with Jesus. The Holy Spirit lives with them and will **continue** to be in them even when the Son has gone away to the Father.

Verses 28–31 have been the cause of much controversy. Opponents of Jesus Christ have often tried to twist these words to make them sound almost as if He were not truly God, almost as if the Father alone were God because He is greater than the Son!

Let's remind ourselves that the Father is greater than the Son **in that the Father is the One Who commands the Son**. There is never a

---

[2] The word Representative perhaps conveys the meaning better than 'Counsellor'.

time when the Father does what the Son commands Him! To even say such a thing makes us shudder. But such a role does not make Him a greater '**being**' than the Son, just as a parent is not a higher level of being to their child. A child is just as human as their parent; a soldier is just as human as his captain. A difference in authority has nothing to do with how human we are. The relationship between the Father and the Son is **the** guarantee of this truth.

The disciples should rejoice that the Son is going back to the Father because it means He **has** accomplished exactly what the Father has commanded Him. The great work of redemption and new creation will be complete when the Son returns to the Father.

4. Remaining in the New Life, 15:1–17

It is abundantly clear that God the Word has made perfect provision for these eleven disciples even though He is leaving them. Now He broadens His teaching to consider their ongoing relationship with Him.

In Psalm 80 and Hosea 10 we see how Israel is a vine. Yet, in both of those passages Israel is a vine that has failed to bear fruit. It has fallen under divine judgement through its sin. Yet, as Psalm 80 prays, there is hope in the Messiah, the Son of Man, who is the **true** Vine.

Psalm 80:16–18: "Your vine is cut down, it is burned with fire; at your rebuke your people perish. Let your hand rest on the Man at your right hand, **the Son of Man** you have raised up for yourself. Then we will not turn away from you; revive us, and we will call on your name."

The hope for the vine of Israel is the **true** Vine, the Son of Man who will make Israel fruitful (John 15:1). This is the great word of encouragement to the disciples (and all believers through history): on our own we will certainly be barren, fruitless and condemned (verse 6), but now that we are connected to the true Vine we are useful, fruitful and established.

If the disciples had been worried about being abandoned when Jesus ascended to the Father, their fears were put to rest. Their lives were organically joined to Jesus the true Vine and God the Father was working **for** them, determined to make the branches really fruitful and useful.

This is the context for verse 7. The goal of life in Jesus is to be fruitful – that is, to be faithful, accurate witnesses to Him (verse 8). As we give ourselves to this task, as do the Father, Son and Holy Spirit, so the Father will give us anything and everything we need. When we read the book of Acts we might be amazed at the power of the Spirit in the lives of the apostles and the other Christians, but we should note the unconditional way in which they gave themselves to the work of witnessing to Jesus. Even against ridicule and severe opposition they continued to pour out their lives so that the world might know Jesus. That is the life of real joy and power. The joy that the Son has in the wonderful love of the Father can be ours also as we follow the commands of Jesus. Jesus does what the Father sends Him to do; and we do what Jesus sends us to do (verses 9–11).

Love is the essence of God, not abstract attributes of power, infinity and knowledge. The disciples of Jesus are His **friends**. He is the Cosmic Word upholding the galaxies, yet those men knew His personal friendship (verse 14) – and so may we, as we also live in the true Vine, following His commands. Jesus did not keep secrets from His friends (verse 15), openly telling them all that the Father told Him. All of these 'secrets' are written in the Scriptures for us, and as we enjoy the friendship of Jesus we will understand all that the Father has revealed through Jesus.

Verse 16 was an important word for those apostles to hear as they faced the great 'mission to the Gentiles' in the coming years. They did not appoint themselves to the task. Jesus had chosen these apostles for the work and when they felt discouraged in later years they would always know that Jesus had selected them for what they were doing. Is the same true for us also? The places we live, work, shop and study are the places where we are known, where we can bear witness to Jesus. Jesus wants each of us to bear fruit under the Father's care in these situations, and as we do so, pursuing that fruitfulness above any other agenda, so we will find our prayers answered in amazing ways (verse 16).

Jesus spoke several times about following His commands. What does He command us to do? In verse 17 we get His command: we are to love each other. We are all branches drawing our life from the true Vine – therefore our life must be a **shared** life, a life of fellowship and love. This is His hardest command, because we naturally only want to love the followers of Jesus who we get on with, who agree with all our doctrinal convictions, who do things just like we do, who have the same social and economic background. That is not love; it is not the love Jesus has shown to us.

Further Questions:

1. Jesus washed the disciples' feet and said (John 13:14) that they should wash each others' feet. Was this intended as a literal command for the disciples to follow, or was it just a metaphor for serving each other? Several Christian groups around the world even today practice foot washing. What benefits would this have for our Christian fellowship? Is car washing a better modern equivalent... or is that too removed from personal contact?

2. Judas is one of the most deeply disturbing characters in the Bible. Jesus chose him as one of the Twelve and none of the other disciples suspected what was going on in Judas' heart and mind (see John 13:29). What is the warning of Judas' life? How could he be so close to Jesus yet so very far from Jesus?

3. John 14:26 has been used in some very unusual ways down the centuries. The apostles were told that the Spirit would remind them of all that Jesus had taught them, yet many have taken it to mean that **they** would be taught further truths by the Spirit. What did Jesus promise to all His followers of every age and what things were just for those apostles who trained under Him at that time?

John chapters 15:18–17:26 – Sending

Key Truth: The Light of the world sends and equips His followers to take the words of eternal life to a world that loves darkness.

Jesus' leaving the world is not the end of His work. Indeed this is only the beginning of the work of preaching the gospel to all nations. That is to be pioneered by the eleven disciples sat in the upper room on that atmospheric evening. Their role will be difficult, but it will be done in the power and presence and under the guidance of the Holy Spirit, who will always be pointing to Jesus.

1. Hatred for the LORD of Life, 15:18–25

Just as Jesus was rejected by the world He created and came to save, so His disciples will be rejected as they hold out the gift of Resurrection life in Him. The world is xenophobic – it hates Jesus and His disciples because they do not belong to it. We have learned from John that the more brightly the Light of the world was shining, the more intense the hatred and hostility against Him.

The disciples cannot expect to be treated any differently than Jesus was. He faced unceasing and terrible persecution, so the disciples cannot expect any better. Whatever teaching the world accepted from Jesus (none), the world will accept from the disciples! Their fate can be no better than His (15:18–20). In an evil irony, the more like Jesus we are, the more hated we will be.

The reason for the world's rejection of Jesus and His followers is that the world rejects God the Father (verse 21). Hatred for Jesus is the same as hatred for the Father, which reminds us that when 'religious' people refuse to follow Jesus they are not showing any respect for the Father at all, no matter how devout or sincere they appear to be.

The amazing signs of Jesus have taken away every possible excuse from the world – so now the guilt of the world is re-affirmed. In verses 22 & 24 Jesus seems to be saying that His teaching and miracles provide an opportunity for the real nature of sin to be manifested. As John 16:9 says, sin is essentially about rejecting Jesus. In His earthly ministry, His liberating teaching and wonderful miracles are absolutely attractive and persuasive. The utter darkness and stupidity of sin is revealed in the world's rejection of Him. Sin is totally irrational – just as Psalm 35:19 prophesied. Psalm 35 is a traumatic Psalm prophesying the spiteful way in which the world would gloat over the Messiah as He died... yet it also prophesied His triumphant vindication at the Resurrection.

2. Witnessing to the LORD of Life, 15:26–16:15

In order to protect them from going astray (16:1) Jesus also reminds His disciples of the great Helper that will always be with them in their work.

Although the Spirit was already with the disciples at that time (verse 17), yet they would receive a special anointing of the Spirit, sent by Jesus from the Father (15:26). The great work of the Spirit is bearing witness to Jesus, so He will be the enthusiastic leader of the work of global evangelism.

The apostles were such good pioneers of this work because they had spent so much time with Jesus, seen all that He had done and listened to all His teaching. They were the authoritative **eye-witnesses** of Jesus.[1]

The great temptation for the disciples (and for the church down the ages) was to keep quiet in their witness to Jesus. Terrible and deluded persecution is coming to the disciples – and it is motivated (just as for Jesus) by an ignorance of the Father (verse 3). The fact that Jesus warned the disciples in advance means that they will not have a crisis when it happens – actually they will be encouraged to trust Jesus more.

It is for the disciples' good that Jesus goes away (verse 7). Jesus is returning to the Father, mission accomplished. From the Father's side He will send the Spirit to equip the disciples for global evangelism. We mustn't take these words of Jesus out of context. We have seen that the Spirit is already with Jesus and His disciples, so Jesus is not speaking as if the Spirit is coming to the world for the first time! Rather, when Jesus ascends as the triumphant King of the universe, so the work of the Spirit will be liberated from the enclosure of the Jews alone. From the day of Pentecost, the Spirit has been poured out on **all flesh**, Jew or Gentile,

[1] In the book of Acts, the key fact about the apostles is that they were **eye-witnesses**.

all over the world. This coming of the Spirit to the whole world was the flood that carried the apostles out over the planet.

Because Jesus is away the Spirit must testify to Jesus as He convicts the world of its darkness and evil (verses 8–11). The world's guilt has three aspects, all of which are focussed on Jesus. The Spirit will convict the world of guilt in regard to:

1. **sin** – for not believing in Jesus. All the sins we commit are symptoms of this disease. People stop their many sins only when they repent of their great sin of unbelief.
2. **righteousness** – because Jesus is with the Father. Jesus is the righteousness of God, and when He is no longer visible it is up to the Spirit to bear witness to Jesus so that the world will know what righteousness really is.
3. **judgement** - because Jesus has defeated the devil. This passing age and its evil ruler has been utterly defeated by the Cross and Resurrection of Jesus. The world needs to know this so that people can escape into the coming age of immortality and light.

Jesus has been cramming a great deal into this final evening. And He has still more to tell them. However, the Spirit of truth will guide them into all the necessary truth when He anoints them for the coming work (verses 12–13). The Spirit will be just as faithful to His mission as Jesus has been to His, passing on only the words given to Him. The Son has been utterly faithful in representing the Father, and so the Spirit will be utterly faithful in representing the Son (verses 14–15).

3. Joy in the LORD of life, 16:16–33

Jesus' humiliating and lonely death at the hands of the Gentile Roman soldiers will leave the disciples feeling alone and in despair. However there is an eternal joy that is sure to follow (verses 16–19). The grief of the Cross will be quickly swallowed up by the joy of the Resurrection (verses 20–22). Just as the pain of labour is quickly forgotten with the joy of a new born baby, so the Resurrection will replace the pain of the Cross. This is the pattern that must sustain all of Jesus' followers as we are ridiculed, rejected and persecuted for speaking about Him. All our present sufferings will be far outweighed by the glory of our Resurrection when Jesus returns.

After the Resurrection the disciples would trust Jesus much more than they did before, verse 23. Although Jesus had consistently told them that He is the Son of the Father, yet they had not prayed to the Father in the name of Jesus. This hesitation would disappear after the Resurrection when they see the complete unity of the Father and the Son. Trusting in Jesus is what gets the ear of the Father in prayer.

After the Resurrection Jesus will use no analogies or parables at all – He will speak plainly about the Father. When we read the apostolic writings we are listening in to that 'plain talking' between the Resurrection and Ascension.

In verses 26–28, Jesus begins to explain the Father to them, assuring them that by trusting in Him the disciples are able to talk **directly** to the Father. Loving Jesus attracts the love of the Father and gives a person an audience in His Most Holy Presence.

The disciples understand this and exuberantly express their pleasure in understanding (verses 29–30). Jesus is pleased for them, but warns them that when the terrible darkness of the Cross comes they would certainly abandon Him, verse 32. Nevertheless they do not need to worry about the Son because He is safely kept in the purposes of the Father. He warns them about this so that they will have peace when they are scattered – but they should not fear that God the Word was being conquered by the world: no, He has already overcome the world even before the Cross.

4. Glory in the LORD of Life, 17:1–26

At last the hour that John has been alluding to throughout his Gospel has arrived. Verse 1 – "**the hour has come**." The hour of total darkness and God-forsakenness is the hour of Jesus' great glory. This will be the most powerful sign of who Jesus is and what He came to do. By the Cross He may grant eternal life to anyone that the Father sends to Him, verse 2. Eternal life is not an abstract kind of immortality. Eternal life is knowing the Father and the Son because that is where real **life** is.[2]

The great burden of this prayer is the perfect unity between the Father and the Son.

Jesus has glorified the Father through His perfect obedience, so now the Father will glorify the Son through the Cross, Resurrection and Ascension, restoring Jesus to the unbroken fellowship that He enjoyed with the Father before the universe existed (verse 5).

In verses 6–8 Jesus tells His Father of the success He has enjoyed in revealing the Father to the disciples. The pinnacle of success for Jesus is that the disciples know for certain that He is **sent** from the Father, that all His words and works are from the Father. In all our presentations of the deity of Jesus, we must always begin and end at this point – Jesus can do

---

[2] John 17:3 is the only time that Jesus refers to Himself as "Jesus Christ".

and say only what the Father gives Him to do and say. This is how the true divinity of Jesus is revealed.

Jesus prays specifically for the eleven disciples who would be the pioneers of global Israel, (verse 9). The Father and the Son share all they have, so these disciples although owned by the Father have glorified the Son. His main request is that the disciples would enjoy the same unity that the Father and the Son enjoy – verse 11. Jesus kept them together while He was with them, but now they must be preserved by the power of His name, given to Him by His Father. His 'name' is His identity and mission. Only Judas was lost… but even this was according to the Father's will, as prophesied in Scripture.

It might seem strange that Jesus talks to the Father as He does in this prayer, telling the Father things that He surely already knows. However, verse 13, the prayer is partly for the benefit of the disciples so that they will know the joy that Jesus always experiences.

The disciples are united to Jesus. This grants them eternal life, personal knowledge of the Father and the joy of Jesus. However, it also means they are hated by the world and face the same kind of treatment as Jesus received (verses 14–16). They cannot be taken out of the world, because their mission is witnessing to the world, so instead Jesus asks for protection for them. The evil one will do all he can to silence the disciples. Jesus asks that they be enabled to keep on witnessing no matter what the devil tries to do.[3]

Rather than conforming to the world to reduce opposition, Jesus prays that the disciples will be even more 'set apart' from the world through the truthful Word of the Father, verse 17. **Set apart** yet **sent out** into the world, following the pattern set by Jesus (verse 19).

Next Jesus looks beyond the eleven to the millions of people who would believe in Him through the global outreach of the apostolic Church. His prayer, again, is that they all be united, just like the Father and the Son (verse 21). Jesus knows that the world will believe as they see the followers of Jesus united in truth, mission and holiness. Christian unity comes as we pursue the evangelistic mission in the way that Jesus has shown us – laying down our lives, whatever the opposition, speaking only what Jesus has told us, doing only what Jesus has sent us to do. Christians become divided as we allow **other** words and works to control us.

---

[3] He doesn't ask that they will be **loved** by the world or that they will face no persecution. Being a comfortable **silent** Christian is victory for the evil one. Whether by pain or pleasure the evil one always wants to silence the Church.

The glory of Jesus is the glory of the Cross. He has shared this with all the believers of history (verse 22), because it is in this faithfulness under persecution that we find real gospel unity. As long as we are caught up in private 'spiritual' agendas we will always argue with each other, but when we are standing under the world's hatred, **then** we need each other and the pure gospel of Jesus too much to fight each other. Pursuing the glory of the Cross is the real road to Church unity.

The Son describes His unity with the Father in terms of unity of word and work. The Father loves the Son because He obeys Him even to the Cross (10:17). The Church is to show the same obedience to His words and example, enjoying the deep, joyful fellowship of the Father and the Son (verse 23). Through the Cross, and only through the Cross, lies the glory of the Resurrection and Ascension. Jesus wants His Church to be with Him in that great glory of the Cross, the glory which shows the eternal love of the Father for the Son. The Cross looks hateful to the world, but to those of us who follow Jesus it is the glorification of Jesus, the exaltation of Jesus over the whole world.

Jesus ends His prayer with a mission statement. The world does not know the Father. Nevertheless Jesus does know the Father and will continue to reveal the Father to the world so that the world may enjoy Jesus' relationship with the Father (verses 25–26). This is the wonder of the gospel that we give our lives to: we are brought into the divine life through Jesus.

Further Questions

1. We are in the world yet set apart from the world. How do we live this out day by day? Many Christians take pride in being as similar to their pagan friends as possible, as if all issues of music, dress, entertainment, money, relationships and career were separate from following Jesus. What is wrong with this approach?

2. Refusing to believe in Jesus is the essence of sin. Sin has many symptoms, such as greed, deceit, sexual immorality, selfishness, violence etc. As we pray for our friends, should we focus on 'sin' or the outward 'sins'? Should our witnessing engage with 'sin' or 'sins'?

3. There are thousands of different churches around the world, all with their own emphases. Some of these 'churches' do not hold to the Biblical gospel at all. Has Jesus' prayer for unity completely failed? Where do we find His gospel unity? How should we relate to the Christians in the different churches in our local area?

John chapters 18-19 – Dying

Key Truth: The death of the Word of God made flesh is the single most significant event in the history of the world, yet the world rejected it.

1. Binding the I AM, 18:1-14, 19-24

After His mighty prayer Jesus crossed the Kidron valley. The keen Bible student will know that this recalls king David leaving Jerusalem when the people rejected him as king (see 2 Samuel 15, especially verse 23). The true King of Israel is also being rejected, so He also symbolically crosses the Kidron valley. However, unlike David, Jesus would not escape from His enemies.

Judas brought a mob to arrest Jesus. When they said they were looking for Jesus He uttered His divine name "I AM" from Exodus 3 and they retreated and fell to the ground (verses 5–6). For a moment their darkness was overwhelmed by His glorious shining presence and they saw, despite their hatred of Him, Who He is and His cosmic authority. Jesus has to speak to them to get them going again (verse 7). Jesus simply asked that His disciples be allowed to go free.

Simon Peter could not bear it and began to trust in the flesh with his sword. John remembered that the man whose ear was cut off was actually called Malchus ('bad ear')! Peter is trying to pursue the option that Jesus rejected back in 12:27. Jesus **must** do what the Father has given Him to do. The moment the followers of Jesus wield the sword[1] they have left His kingdom behind and joined the kingdoms of the world.

Jesus is firstly taken to Annas (verse 13), who was nothing but the father-in-law of Caiaphas the high priest. It seems that he had kept his

---

[1] In this connection, it is important to remember how Jesus regarded verbal and mental violence as murder. See Matthew 5:21–22.

high priestly influence even though his son-in-law had the official position. Peter could only get as far as the outside courtyard (verses 15–16), but John (presumably) had connections to get them right inside to watch what happened.

Annas questioned Jesus, but Jesus simply referred him to His own public teaching (verses 19–21). He was not going to give private tutorials to this mafia thug. We are shocked by verse 22, that God the Word, the LORD Almighty, the beloved Son of the Father is struck **in the face** for not being respectful to this Annas criminal. Once again Jesus refused to be intimidated by violence, verses 22–23, so He was sent to the official high priest, Caiaphas.

2. Denying the I AM, 18:15–18, 25–27

Meanwhile, Peter faces a similar test. Was Peter sanctified, set apart from the world and committed only to Jesus? Could He stand with God the Word when the powers of darkness are given their hour?

Peter still had the courage to wait outside the door as the forces of darkness gathered around Jesus, but he had no real strength at that time – and even a little girl intimidated him so much that he denied knowing Jesus. The contrast with verse 5 is strong: "I AM" and "I am NOT".

Peter warmed himself at the fire, a detail John wants us to remember. We will see Peter at another fire before very long.

3. Judging the I AM, 18:28–19:16

It was early morning and Jesus was taken to Pilate. Verse 28 is outrageous – they didn't want to be ceremonially unclean for Passover as they murdered the very One Who had delivered them out of the land of Egypt. It was the One sent from the LORD (the Angel of the LORD – see Judges 2:1–4) who had performed the original Passover, and now He was rejected in favour of the mere ceremony. How typical of the wicked, unbelieving human heart! Religion will always come before reality in our rebellion against Jesus.

Pilate is not impressed with the flimsy and drummed up nature of the charges against Jesus (verses 28–31). The Jews won't leave Pilate though because only the Romans held the legal right of execution. Jesus had prophesied that He would die by crucifixion, so it all had to happen this way.

Pilate had some idea of the 'case' because he had heard that Jesus claimed to be the King of the Jews (verse 33). Jesus knew that Pilate was being set up by others, and acknowledged this. Jesus effectively rejected the accusation, defining His kingdom as belonging to 'another place'. This is so important. At no point did Jesus ever indicate that He was interested in the kind of empires and kingdoms that the world pursues. He rejected Peter's military empire of verse 10, precisely because His Kingdom belonged to the coming age of the Resurrection and not to this passing age of darkness and death.

Pilate pounced on the word 'king', which Jesus affirms. When Jesus said that everybody on the side of truth listens to Him, Pilate with the weary worldly wisdom of the cynic asks 'what is truth?' Truth was standing right in front of him (14:6), yet Pilate didn't wait for an answer. When people talk about "looking for the truth" we can always detect how serious they are by their reaction to the Person who actually is The Truth.

Pilate could see that Jesus was innocent, and thinks about the custom of releasing a prisoner at Passover (verses 38–39). He wants an easy way out of the mess. The crowd formally reject Jesus as their king. It was early morning, so where had this crowd come from? Who had organised the Jerusalem people to express their hatred of Jesus? Right from John 1:19 we have seen the religious leadership in Jerusalem organising opposition to Jesus and His friends.

Bar-abbas (son of father) was chosen instead of Jesus, the true Son of **the** Father (verse 40). Barabbas belonged to the darkness and was far more attractive to them.

Pilate had no passion for justice or truth so he had Jesus flogged (19:1). What evil and arrogant cruelty! The soldiers decide to make a mockery of the King, with the crown of thorns and purple robe. Again, verse 3, He was struck in the face, showing their determination to humiliate the Living God.

Once more Pilate hoped to placate the crowd having unjustly abused an innocent man. Verse 5 is his famous saying in the Latin translations "ecce homo!" – "behold The Man!" Yet, as soon as the priests and their officials saw the Lamb of God they howled for His death.

Pilate won't go along with this, but the crowd insist because "He claimed to be the Son of God" (verse 7). This disturbs Pilate and he wants to know more. He trembles at thought of murdering the everlasting Word who upholds the universe. He had mocked and insulted Jesus and now Jesus would give him no answer.

The fact that Pilate had flogged Jesus **knowing** that Jesus was innocent showed that Pilate was a deeply evil man who had no interest in the truth of Jesus at all. Pilate knew all that he needed to know and now he must decide whether he will 'live' in the death of unbelief or die with Jesus in the glory of eternal life. It is the decision that we all face and Pilate retreats into the darkness.

He tried to boast of his authority, but Jesus puts him in his place (verse 11). Pilate is shaken by that and tries even harder to have Jesus released. If he really had all the authority he had boasted of, why can't he simply let Jesus go?! He had no power at all. When the crowd threatened Pilate with his own god, Caesar, he gave in. He held Caesar to be far more important than the Son of God.

Pilate brought Jesus out to the place of judgement on the day of preparation (verses 13–14). There is a strange significance to this. Jesus was **the** Passover Lamb being prepared for sacrifice. No fault is found in Him. He is an **unblemished** Lamb, and the crowd cry out for Him to be killed.

Pilate questions the crowd and discovers that they want to formally reject even the pretence of the LORD as the King of Israel (verse 15). When Isaiah met Jesus in Isaiah chapter 6 (see John 12:41), he acknowledged Him to be the King, but this crowd acknowledge no king but a pagan Gentile tyrant. They prefer Pilate's god, Caesar, to the LORD God of Israel.

4. Killing the I AM, 19:17–42

The LORD of life carries His own cross to the place of death, accompanied by two criminals. Pilate wanted the world to know that Jesus was the King of the Jews, and resisted the attempts of the chief priests to change this (verses 19–22). Why did he do this? If he understood in some way the true identity of Jesus, then it seems strange to allow Him to be murdered. It seems more likely that he wanted to be able to claim to have put down a Jewish rebellion the next time he reported back to Caesar.

At so many points John makes us aware that even in this evil reign of darkness, everything is under the sovereign control of the Father. So (verses 22–24) the soldiers cast lots to take Jesus' clothing, just as the Scriptures prophesied in Psalm 22:18.

Mary had been warned about this time when Jesus had been a little baby. Luke 2:34–35 "Simeon blessed them and said to Mary, His mother: 'This child is destined to cause the falling and rising of many in Israel, and to be a sign that will be spoken against, so that the thoughts of many hearts will be revealed. And a sword will pierce your own soul too.'" As she stood by the cross with her friends and relatives this prophecy too was fulfilled. Yet, even then in His agony, Jesus cares for His mother. John seemed to have remained with Jesus right through the trial and now through His death, and John is given the responsibility of looking after Mary from this time on (verses 25–27).

The thirst of Jesus (verse 28) gathers up this mighty theme from John. The Fount of Living Water had run dry. He was cut off from the Father's source of life, tormented in His God-forsaken desolation. The eternal Son, God the Word, experienced what He had never known before: He was cut off from the joy and fellowship of the divine life. Again this happened to fulfil just what the Scriptures had prophesied about Him.

To further torment Him the crowd tried to give Him vinegar, another cruelty prophesied in the Scriptures (Psalm 69:21). The Psalms are full of these Messianic prophesies, detailing the ways in which He would suffer in His great work. John wants us to see what a wonderful proof this is of all that Jesus did and said. Who other than the divine Mediator is spoken of in such specific and intentional detail hundreds of years earlier?

Jesus was given the vinegar on the end of a hyssop plant, which was presumably being used in the Passover celebrations (see Exodus 12:21–23). The hyssop plant was originally used to apply the blood of the Passover lamb to each household. You would have thought that the hyssop plant would have made these people think about applying the blood of the true Passover Lamb to themselves, rather than tormenting Him with it.

Then Jesus said "**it is finished**". What is finished? He has finished what He had been sent to do. The mighty work that the Father gave Him to do, the judgement of the world, atonement for sin and the overthrow of Satan was all finished. It is a mighty moment because it reminds us that there is nothing for **us** to finish in our salvation. The work of salvation is **His** work and **He** finished it on our behalf. Furthermore, this cry of Jesus tells us that there was nothing more for Him to do to make atonement. He did not have to go to the lake of fire to continue to suffer after His death. No, as Luke 23:43 tells us, as soon as He died He went to paradise, having completed the work of atonement.

To avoid defiling the Sabbath they wanted to make sure they had killed the LORD of the Sabbath (verse 31). The two criminals were finished off, but Jesus was already dead. So, instead, the soldiers pierced His side, fulfilling the prophecy of Zechariah 12:10 when the LORD God says "they will look on **Me**, the One they have pierced."

The great 18th century Bible scholar Matthew Henry makes this observation, recalling the events of Genesis 2:21–24: "When Christ, the second Adam, was fallen into a 'deep sleep' upon the cross, then was His side opened, and out of it was His Church taken, which He espoused to Himself. See Ephesians 5:30, 32."

It was crucial that none of Jesus' bones were broken (verse 36). Right from the original Passover in the book of Exodus, it was prophesied that the Lamb of God would not have any of His bones broken – Exodus 12:46. See also Numbers 9:12 and Psalm 34:20.

Joseph of Arimathea, a secret disciple of Jesus, arranged with Pilate to take Jesus' body and Nicodemus, who was clearly now born again, came to anoint the body of Jesus. Some have thought that their desire to anoint His body showed that they didn't believe that He would be resurrected. Why waste so much time and money when Jesus would be raised on the third day? However, it seems better to see their work as a sign of their great devotion and reverence for Jesus, indicating that they expected this body to be raised to life.

"They showed not only the charitable respect of committing His body to the earth, but the honourable respect shown to great men. This they might do, and yet believe and look for His Resurrection; nay, this they might do in the belief and expectation of it. Since God designed honour for this body, they would put honour upon it." (Matthew Henry).

Further Questions:

1. Jesus commanded Peter not to wield the sword in His name. Few Christians today would want to support anything like the medieval crusades, but what kinds of 'worldly' power do we want to use to defend and support the kingdom of Jesus? Do we believe in using legislation to enforce Christian behaviour on unbelievers? Would we take up weapons to defend ourselves if we were being persecuted? Do we want our government to intervene to protect the persecuted church in other countries?

2. If the Living God is the Father, Son and Holy Spirit, how can the Father forsake the Son on the Cross? How can God still exist when the Son is thirsty for the Father's presence? How would you try to explain this to an enquirer? What Scriptures are the most helpful?

3. Joseph and Nicodemus put a lot of care into the burial of Jesus' body as part of their confidence in His Resurrection. What about our own burial practices? How do they show our Resurrection hope? Do we need to develop different practices? Is cremation any different than burial?

John chapters 20–21 – Living

Key Truth: Jesus is the Resurrected LORD of the New Creation and if we believe in Him we have life.

1. The Empty Tomb, 20:1–9

When it was still dark on Sunday morning Mary Magdelene went to see the tomb. Why? Did she want to see if He had been resurrected just as He had predicted? When she saw the stone rolled away she feared that the enemies had stolen Him (verse 2). Peter and John came running to see, probably full of questions and possibly full of doubts. John got there first and saw the burial linen lying in the tomb. Their owner was not wearing them!

When Peter arrived he looked in, **saw and believed**. John realises that it should not have required visual confirmation before they believed that Jesus had been raised from the dead, so in verse 9 he explains that they had ignored the Scriptures that had spoken of Jesus' Resurrection. We must remember that a lack of understanding is not innocent ignorance in the Gospels; it is a consequence of unbelief and hard-heartedness.

2. Appearing to His Disciples, 20:10–31

Peter and John went home, but Mary remained weeping. Two angels had arrived, perhaps to guard the place of the Resurrection, perhaps to provide instruction to any early worshippers. For **them** it is a day of great joy, so they wonder why she is crying (verse 13). Surely this must be the happiest day of her life! She is confused and assumes that the body has been stolen, even though Peter and John believe.

When she turned around Jesus was standing there, but she didn't recognise Him at first. Perhaps her tears clouded her vision, or maybe she was looking at the ground in her sorrow. It may also have been like the disciples on the road to Emmaus in Luke 24 who were miraculously **prevented** from recognising Jesus (Luke 24:16) until He was ready. There is certainly no suggestion that Jesus looked physically different.

John notes that Mary thought that He was the gardener. Knowing John as we do, it is quite possible that he wants us to remember Jesus in the Garden of Eden way back in Genesis chapters 2 and 3. Jesus **was** the Gardener!

As soon as He spoke her name she recognised Him. She cried out in recognition expressing her great love for Him, and it seems that she hugged Him tightly in her joy (verse 17). Jesus gently tells her that she must not cling onto Him too much because He is not going to be around permanently as He was before. Jesus had done what the Father had sent Him to do. After 40 days He would ascend to the Father, beyond the physical reach of the disciples. Mary and the disciples had to realise that things were going to be different now. They had to prepare themselves for His absence.

In the evening of that first day the disciples had gathered together (verse 19), probably discussing and arguing and rejoicing in all that had happened – What had really occurred? Who had seen what? When did it happen? What did He look like? Where are the grave clothes? Who had been to see? etc.

They had closed[1] the door because they were still frightened of the forces of darkness.

Jesus came into the room and gave them His peace (remember John 14:27). With those words any remaining confusion or agitation would have been driven away. He showed them His wounds. They were overjoyed. It was all as the Scriptures had so clearly predicted; just as Jesus Himself had told them. It must have been such an amazingly happy time. Was it like Jesus had said in 16:21 – was the pain of the Cross forgotten in the wonderful euphoric joy of the New Creation? Jesus must have so enjoyed this time of celebration after the heavy work He had accomplished.

Standing among the disciples was the future of the universe. They could see exactly what the future looked like... and it was physical resurrection to immortality. All the vague and ethereal hopes of mere

---

[1] The Greek does not necessarily mean they **locked** the door. Some assume that Jesus walked through the wall in a ghostly way, but He may just as well have opened the door and walked into the room.

religion seem so insubstantial and tasteless compared to this – the Risen Jesus standing in His incorruptible **physical** body celebrating with His disciples.

The disciples were looking at and examining their own future – they saw what the future of the whole creation looked like. They could touch it and handle it. Their laughter and joy were driving away the darkness, and they would never look back.

Again He gave them His peace (verse 21) and reminds them that He is sending them just as the Father had sent Him. This is vital. They had seen that **His** faithfulness in accomplishing the will of the Father had been utterly vindicated. This joy and immortal life was waiting for them also in the Resurrection future. So just as Jesus had set His hope on this future joy, so must the disciples. They had seen that His obedience to His mission was all worthwhile in the Resurrection, so they too could lay down their lives in obedience as they were sent out, knowing that the joy of the Resurrection future would far surpass any pain or loss they suffered now.

He breathed on them the Breath of God, the Holy Spirit (verse 22). It seems likely that this was a promise or guarantee of the great anointing for service that they would receive on the Day of Pentecost. They would all remember all their lives the warm Breath of the Living God upon them on that Resurrection Morning.

He also gives them His authority, the authority of the gospel, verse 23. By the gospel the Church is able to accurately pronounce the forgiveness of sins. By the gospel we are able to declare a person's sins forgiven or not, according to whether they trust in Jesus or not. If we speak to a person and they admit that they do not trust in Jesus then we have the authority of heaven itself to tell them that their sins are certainly not forgiven. On the other hand when we meet a Christian who is full of fear, when they tell us that they trust in Jesus we can reassure them with the authority of heaven that their sins are certainly forgiven.

Thomas the Twin[2] had missed out on that wonderful celebration, but when he met the others who were bubbling over with excitement about meeting Jesus, he refused to come into the light. He was sinful in his unbelief. Jesus had told them very plainly that He would be raised from the dead, and Thomas won't even consider it even when the eye-witnesses report the reality of the Resurrection.

In the 18th century West (and even today) doubt was considered a good thing. Thomas was often held up as a kind of hero who refused to believe in the Resurrection without "scientific proof". That is **not** how John regards Thomas' evil unbelief.

---

[2] Who is he the twin of? John thinks it is worth telling us that he was a twin, but why?

Jesus visits them again a week later (verse 26).[3] He gives them His peace again and confronts Thomas with his request for physical evidence. Thomas is rebuked for doubting – "stop doubting and believe." Jesus explains why Thomas is a bad example for the Church down the ages. He insisted on walking by **sight** and not by trusting Jesus. There would be a few hundred believers who were able to physically inspect the Resurrection body of Jesus. Hundreds of millions of believers down the ages have trusted the Scriptures and the eye-witness reports of the apostles. Jesus said that there is **blessing** in being among those who trust the Scriptures rather than being like doubting Thomas.

Thomas, to his credit, does make a reasonable confession of faith – "My LORD and My God." From his sinful unbelief he bursts into a victorious confession of Jesus' identity.[4]

Verses 30–31 summarise the whole book of John. The purpose of everything John has written is to bring us to believe that Jesus is the prophesied Messiah, the Son of God. As we trust ourselves to Jesus in this way, so we receive life in His name. It is true that this has been the overwhelming theme of all that we have read in this Gospel and it seems impossible for anyone not to believe.

3. The Miraculous Catch, 21:1-14

On another day Jesus visited the disciples again. It seems they didn't quite know what to do with themselves. Everything had changed and yet their lives were just the same – what next? What to do? So they decided to do some fishing. They had done that sort of thing with Jesus many times and it was their profession (verse 3).

They went out at night and caught nothing. Early in the morning Jesus stood on the shore, but they didn't recognise Him. He performed a miracle of allowing them to catch a huge quantity of fish, and this allowed John to recognise Jesus (verse 7). Peter was so overjoyed at this that he simply jumped into the water and swam for the shore, leaving the others to struggle with the fish.

Jesus had made a fire for them. There were two reasons for this. First, it would recall to Peter the night that he betrayed Jesus. As Peter sat

---

[3] Where had Jesus been for that week? There has been much speculation. Was He spending time with His mother Mary? Was He visiting other believers? Perhaps He returned to Paradise, although this would seem strange given His imminent ascension.

[4] We must simply laugh at the suggestion from the Jehovah's Witnesses that Thomas is blasphemously swearing at this point.

dripping wet, warming himself by this fire, surely the smell of the fire would have brought it all back to him. Peter must have felt so deeply ashamed of what he had done. Jesus would take time to restore him.

The second reason for the fire was more practical. Jesus was cooking breakfast for the disciples. He was serving them as they rested from their fishing trip. There is something so completely **normal** about this scene – a group of men enjoying an early morning breakfast together. Yet, one of these men had just passed through death into the incorruptible life of the New Creation! Here we get such a wonderful glimpse of the life we will enjoy on the renewed earth after Resurrection Morning. We will enjoy life on earth as it was always supposed to be in the glorious company of the Father, Son and Holy Spirit. We should think about this every day.

4. Commissioning Peter, 21:15-25

After breakfast (verse 15), Jesus began to restore Peter. Peter had denied Jesus three times so he is given three opportunities to re-affirm his love for Jesus. The question seems slightly ambiguous to us. Does Peter love Jesus more than he loves the other disciples? Does Peter love Jesus more than the other disciples love Jesus? Does Peter love Jesus more than the fish.. or the world generally? Whatever is the exact nuance of the question, Peter's answer shows us what Jesus is **really** asking.

Do you love me?	Lord I love you	Feed my lambs
Do you truly love me?	Lord I love you	Take care of my sheep
Do you love me?	Lord I love you	Feed my sheep

Jesus responds to Peter's declarations of love in three slightly different ways. It seems that Peter is granted more responsibility with each answer, from feeding lambs to feeding sheep. The key point is that Jesus repetitively affirms Peter as an apostle. Peter was not cut off from the team because of his sin.

Peter had loved his own safety and comfort more than Jesus. When the pressure was on he didn't want to be associated with Jesus. This was not unique to Peter. It is the constant temptation for followers of Jesus facing the opposition that the world will always present us with. When we read Peter's epistles we see how deeply these lessons were burned onto his heart and mind as he shows us how to stand firm under persecution.

Peter would be able to glorify God just as Jesus Himself had done (verses 18–19).[5] He would be given the great privilege of crucifixion. All his life Peter knew that a day would come when he would be asked the same kind of questions that he had been asked at the high priest's fire. Jesus prophesied that when that day came he would not deny Him and would be allowed to share in the sufferings of Jesus.

John knows that all that he has written is true (verse 24), but he doesn't want us to think that he has exhausted the subject of Jesus. He has shown us that Jesus is greater and older than the whole universe. We will spend everlasting ages learning more and more about Him, discovering more and more of what He has done.

Epilogue: There is a real treat in store for us after we have read and studied John's Gospel as we have just done. We have spent our time tuning into the wonders and challenges of the great apostle John's inspired Gospel... but now we can turn to his epistles at the end of the Bible. Having learned so much about what John means, how he understood God the Word, these epistles are such a thrill to read. Just listen to this little sample from 1 John 5:11–12 – "This is the testimony: God has given us eternal life, and this life is in His Son. He who has the Son has life; he who does not have the Son of God does not have life." These words should make us gasp for more!

---

[5] We must note again in verse 19 the connection that John makes between death and glory. To suffer or die for the name of Jesus brings great glory to God.

Further Questions

1. John writes about Resurrection life in such earthy, physical terms. He allows us to glimpse new creation life as **this** life with all the death, pain and sin removed. Is this how we think about our Resurrection future? Why do Christians sometimes speak about "dying and going to heaven forever" almost as if they didn't believe in a physical earthly Resurrection at the return of Jesus?

2. Many of us spend a lot of time trying to present the gospel in ways that will cause the minimum offence and conflict with the world. John's Gospel has shown us that there is a sharp and hostile conflict between light and darkness. How should this change the way we interact with the world around us? Should it change the way we view our Christian and non-Christian friends?

3. John has been called "the Theologian" because he has so much to say about the doctrine of God. In the light of our studies, do you think it is possible (even for just a moment) to speak about God without talking about Jesus?